Instant Immersion™

Japanese

© 2003 Topics Entertainment, Inc.
1600 S.W. 43rd Street, Renton, WA 98055 U.S.A.
www.topics–ent.com

developed by Mary March, M.A.

written by Meghan Barstow

ISBN 1–59150–311–6

edited by AOLTI
Creative Director: Tricia Vander Leest
Illustrations by Elizabeth Haidle
Art Director: Paul Haidle
Design by Paul Haidle
Maps by Lonely Planet®

Printed on 100% recycled paper. Printed in the U.S.A.

TABLE OF CONTENTS

INTRODUCTION

Yōkoso (welcome) to *Instant Immersion Japanese™!* An understanding of other cultures is critical in becoming part of a larger global community. Knowing how to communicate in other languages is one way to facilitate this process. Japan, a country rich in culture and tradition, has long been a source of fascination for Westerners. The country offers the casual tourist or student abundant opportunities to observe architecture, religion, food, dress, and traditional arts that are uniquely Japanese. Japan has also become an economic powerhouse, with the second largest economy in the world. The country is a world leader in innovative technology and modern art forms such as animation and graphic design. An understanding of Japanese will enhance a visit to Japan, or your interaction with Japanese people you meet in your country. Whether you are interested in Japan for business, tourism, or study, ability to communicate in the language will open doors into this intriguing culture that might otherwise remain closed and unexplored.

Japanese has earned a reputation as a difficult language to master. While the written language and the complicated social hierarchy do challenge beginners, pronunciation and basic grammar are quite easy for English speakers. Additionally, Japanese are delighted when a visitor has taken the time and effort to learn even a few phrases and are extremely receptive to a beginner's efforts. Opportunities to practice the Japanese you have learned in this book will abound in the countryside in Japan, and even in the bigger cities where many Japanese are hesitant to use the English they learned in school. So this textbook is the first step in what we hope will be a long and fruitful discovery of Japan and the Japanese language.

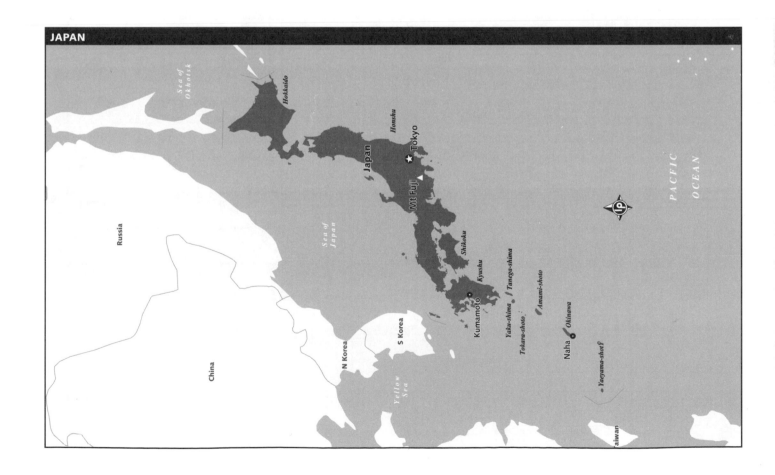

JAPANESE: THE LANGUAGE OF MANY LETTERS

Japanese uses a combination of three writing systems: hiragana, katakana, and kanji.

Hiragana and katakana are alphabets representing 46 different syllables. Both katakana and hiragana represent the same sounds. Hiragana is used for native Japanese words (e.g., "gohan" for rice-), and katakana represents words "borrowed" from other countries. (e.g., "pan" for bread, which came from Portuguese traders).

Kanji characters, imported from China in the fourth or fifth century, are symbols or pictures that represent words and sounds. The average Japanese person knows more than 2,000 kanji, the bare minimum necessary to read a newspaper.

These three systems can all be used in the same sentence. For example, "Japanese bread is delicious" can be written as follows: 日本　の　パン　は　美味しい　です。

日本 (kanji)　の(hiragana)　パン (katakana)　は (hiragana)　美味 (kanji)　しいです (hiragana)

In addition, to simplify reading Japanese for non-natives, a writing system called Romaji has been developed that represents the Japanese scripts in a western alphabet. This Romaji script is used in this book, but you may want to learn some hiragana or katakana in order to navigate a train station or a menu. These two scripts are introduced below.

HIRAGANA
ひらがな

あ – a ma	い - i key	う - u move	え – e hay	お – o oh no
か- ka call	き- ki key	く -ku cool	け-ke okay	こ-ko cone
さ-sa sat	し-shi she	す-su sue	せ-se cent	そ-so sew
た-ta tap	ち-chi cheat	つ-tsu t+sue	て-te table	と-to toe
な-na nice	に ni neat	ぬ-nu new	ね –ne neighbor	の-no nose
は-ha hah hah	ひ-hi he	ふ-fu full	へ –he hen	ほ-ho horse
ま-ma ma	み-mi me	む-mu moon	め-me mess	も-mo morning
や- ya yard		ゆ- yu you		よ- yo yodel
ら- ra rabbit	り - ri ring	る –ru loser	れ- re race	ろ –ro robot
わ- wa water				を- o/ wo oh/woe
ん- n siren				

きゃ-kya kyah	きゅ-kyu kyoo	きょ-kyo kyoh
しゃ-sha shine	しゅ-shu shoe	しょ-sho show
ちゃ-cha charm	ちゅ-chu choo	ちょ-cho choke
にゃ-nya nyah	にゅ-nyu nyoo	にょ-nyo nyoh
ひゃ-hya hyah	ひゅ-hyu hyoo	ひょ-hyo hyoh
みゃ-mya myah	みゅ-my myoo	みょ-myo myoh

りゃ –rya ryah	りゅ-ryu ryoo	りょ –ryo ryoh

が –ga garden	ぎ –gi doggy	ぐ- gu goon	げ- ge gate	ご- go go away

ぎゃ- gya gyah	ぎゅ- gyu gyoo	ぎょ-gyo gyoh

ざ- za Zah	じ-ji gee whiz	ず- zu zoom	ぜ- ze zen	ぞ- zo zone
だ-da daunting	ぢ-ji gee whiz	づ-zu zoo	で-de date	ど-do don`t
ば –ba bark	び –bi beak	ぶ –bu book	べ- be bench	ぼ- bo bore
ぱ -pa popcorn	ぴ –pi piece	ぷ- pu poodle	ぺ- pe page	ぽ –po poem

じゃ- ja jyah	じゅ-ju jyoo	じょ- jo jyoh

びゃ -bya byah	びゅ- byu byoo	びょ- byo byoh
ぴゃ -pya pyah	ぴゅ –pyu pyoo	ぴょ -pyo pyoh

KATAKANA
カタカナ

This second syllabary system represents the same 46 syllables that are in hiragana. Compare the character for *"ka"* in both alphabets. Can you see the subtle difference? Katakana tends to be more angular than hiragana.

ア – a	イ - i	ウ- u	エ- e	オ – o
カ- ka	キ- ki	ク-ku	ケ-ke	コ-ko
サ-sa	シ-shi	ス-su	せ-se	ソ-so
タ-ta	チ-chi	ツ-tsu	テ-te	ト-to
ナ-na	ニ ni	ヌ-nu	ネ –ne	ノ -no
ハ-ha	ヒ-hi	フ-fu	へ –he	ホ-ho
マ-ma	ミ-mi	ム-mu	メ-me	モ-mo
ヤ- ya		ユ- yu		ヨ- yo
ラ-ra	リ-ri	ル –ru	レ- re	ロ –ro
ワ- wa				ヲ- o/ wo
ン - n				

キャ-kya	キュ-kyu	キョ-kyo
シャ-sha	シュ-shu	ショ-sho
チャ-cha	チュ-chu	チョ-cho
ニャ-nya	ニュ-nyu	ニョ-nyo
ヒャ-hya	ヒュ-hyu	ヒョ-hyo
ミャ mya	ミュ myu	ミョ myo

リャ rya	リュ ryu	リョ ryo

ガ –ga	ギ-gi	グ- gu	ゲ-ge	ゴ- go
ザ- za	ジ-ji	ズ-zu	ゼ-ze	ゾ-zo
だ-da	ヂ-ji	ヅ-zu	デ-de	ど-do
バ –ba	ビ-bi	ブ-bu	べ-be	ボ- bo
パ -pa	ピ-pi	プ- pu	ぺ-pe	ポ –po

ギャ- gya	ギュ -gyu	ギョ -gyo
ジャ -ja	ジュ ju	ジョ -jo

ビャ -bya	ビュ-byu	ビョ-byo
ピャ-pya	ピュ -pyu	ピョ -pyo

Instant Immersion Japanese™ has 16 chapters. It is best to work through the book chapter by chapter, building on an understanding of the grammar. However, vocabulary is cross-referenced in the glossary so you may choose to study by topic of interest. Study the expressions and vocabulary before reading the dialog or story. Say them out loud to practice your pronunciation. Read the dialog or story as many times as you need for understanding. Then read it out loud. Check your answers to the exercises in the Answer Key in the back of the book.

CHAPTER 1

Ohayō Gozaimasu
Good morning!

Pronunciation is the easiest part in learning Japanese, with only a few sounds that are difficult for non-native speakers. Japanese is based on syllables that always, with the exception of n, end in a vowel. These syllables are all based on the building block vowels in the Japanese language: 'a' is in ma, 'i' as in key, 'u' as in move, 'e' as in bet, 'o' as in on. Syllables are usually evenly emphasized and monosyllabic.

Japanese draws on many set phrases to express sentiments or ideas that are universally accepted as correct. Once you memorize the set phrases, or expressions, you sound fluent! Each chapter will introduce two or more new idioms. Try to learn all of them and you will know at least 40 by the end of this book!

Nan de mo ī desu.
Anything is fine with me.

Ikimashō.
Let's go.

otoko no hito
man

asa
morning

onna no hito
woman

hanashimasu
to speak

issho ni
together

ohisashiburi
long time no see

ikimasu
go

ohayō gozaimasu
Good Morning

furansu pan
french bread

tabemasu
eat

hoshī
want (noun)

hiru gohan
lunch

ban gohan
dinner

asa gohan
breakfast

DIALOG

Asa desu. Onna no hito *(Azuma san)* to otoko no hito
and
(Konishi san) ga isshoni hanashite imasu.
are talking

Ms. Azuma: Konishi san, ohayō gozaimasu.

Ohisashiburi desu ne.

Mr. Konishi: Sō desu ne. Ohisashiburi desu ne.
That's right/that's so

Ms. Azuma: Asa gohan wa doko de tabemasu ka.
where at

Mr. Konishi: Doko demo ī desu. Kissaten
café
wa dō desu ka.
how about?

Watashi wa furansupan to furūtsu ga hoshī desu.
fruit

Ms. Azuma: Watashi mo furansupan ga hoshī desu.
Me too

Jā, ikimashō!
well, then

PRACTICE

asa gohan	tabemasu	hiru gohan	ka
de	ban gohan	doko	

Fill in the blanks using the words in the box.

1. _____ wa doko de _____ ka. *8 p.m.*

2. _____ wa doko _____ tabemasu ka. *8 a.m.*

3. _____ wa doko de tabemasu _____ . *12:00 noon*

4. _____ de tabemasu ka.

MATCHING

Match the sentence with the picture.

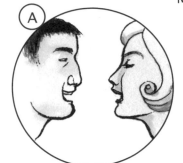

_____ 1. Otoko no hito to onna no hito ga hanashite imasu.

_____ 2. Watashi mo. Ikimashō!

_____ 3. Nan de mo ī desu.

_____ 4. Asa desu.

_____ 5. Kissaten de asagohan o tabemasu.

_____ 6. Furūtsu ga hoshī desu.

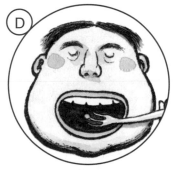

SUBJECT PRONOUNS

	SINGULAR		PLURAL
_I/me_	watashi	_we/us_	watashi tachi
(formal)	watakushi		
(male)	boku		
you	anata	_you (plural)_	anatatachi
		(formal)	anatagata
he/him	kare	_they/them (m/f)_	karera
she/her	kanojo	_they/them (f)_	kanojotachi
			kanojora

VERB CONJUGATIONS

taberu
to eat

Watashi wa sukoshi tabemasu.
I eat a little.

Watashitachi wa takusan tabemasu.
We eat a lot.

Tanaka san wa niku o tabemasu.
Mr. Tanaka eats meat.

Watashitachi wa pasuta o tabemasu.
We eat pasta.

Sensē wa kuruma no naka de tabemasu.
The teacher eats inside of the car.

Kanojotachi wa bīchi de tabemasu.
They eat on the beach.

Onīsan wa bīchi de tabemasu.
The elder brother eats on the beach.

Karera wa beddo de tabemasu.
They eat in bed.

1. Japanese sentence structure, unlike English and other romance languages, is SOV (Subject Object Verb). The verb, or a verb form, comes at the end of the sentence and modifications to the verb come before it. Ex: *Asagohan wa doko de tabemasu ka* literally is: *Breakfast where at eat*

2. Japanese verbs do not need to agree with the subject. Nor do they change to show number or gender.

3. There are only two basic verb tenses, past and present. There is no future form of the verb. The two basic tenses you will see are masu (present or future) and mashita (past tense). In addition, other conjugations and forms are used to express feeling, intent, and politeness.

    Furansu pan o tabemasu.   (I) eat or will eat french bread
    Furansu pan o tabemashita.   (I) ate french bread

TABERU
to eat

Verb endings can be changed to give the verb a new meaning. Every Japanese verb has a stem, which remains the same or changes very little. Notice the verb endings introduced below and try to recognize them when they are introduced with other verbs in following chapters.

Stem
tabe + masu   *eat*
tabe + mashita   *ate*
tabe + ni+ ikimasu   *go to eat*
tabe + mashō   *let's eat*
tabe + te + imasu   *eating*

Note: *'Taberu'* is the infinitive form of the verb. This is the verb form you will find in the dictionary. It is also called the 'plain form', because *'taberu'* is used instead of *'tabemasu'* in plain, informal speech.

Here are some useful expressions with *taberu*.

Watashi wa takusan tabemashita.   *I ate a lot.*
            a lot

Boku wa sutēki o tabetai desu.   *I want to eat steak.*
        steak

Ban gohan o issho ni tabe ni ikimasu ka.   *Will you go eat dinner with me?*

Sushi o tabemashō.   *Let's eat sushi!*

Kinoshita san wa hiru gohan o tabete imasu.   *Ms. Kinoshita is eating lunch.*

CHAPTER 2

Onaka ga suite imasu.
I'm hungry!

Reading Japanese will help you learn how to understand the language. It is an easy, effective way to increase your vocabulary and knowledge of grammatical structures. Practice saying the idioms and vocabulary words. Study the meaning of each. Then read the story silently, trying to understand it. Read the story again out loud, focusing on the pronunciation of the words.

Yokatta.
What luck! / That's great.

(Watashi wa) onaka ga suite imasu.
I'm hungry.

VOCABULARY

hairimasu
enter

demasu
leave

ureshī
happy

kanashī
sad

tomodachi
friends

chīzu
cheese

agemasu
give

NUMBERS

Try to memorize the numbers 0–10 now (Practice counting throughout the day!) and more numbers will be introduced in later chapters.

0	1	2	3	4	5
zero	ichi	ni	san	shi/yon	go

6	7	8	9	10	
roku	nana/shichi	hachi	kyū/ku	jū	

PRACTICE

Write the answers to these simple arithmetic problems in words.

1. san + ichi = _____

2. roku + yon = _____

3. ni + san = _____

4. hachi – go = _____

5. kyū – hachi = _____

6. jū – san = _____

7. yon x ni = _____

8. san x san = _____

STORY

Satomi to tomodachi no Fumiko wa resutoran ni imasu.
and   restaurant   in   to be

Satomi wa chīzu sandoicchi o tabete imasu.
sandwich

Fumiko wa chīzu sandoicchi o futatsu motte imasu.
2 objects   to have

Tomo ga resutoran ni hairimasu.
into

Satomi wa Fumiko ni Tomo o shōkai shimasu.
to   introduce

Tomo: "Hajimemasite. Dōzo yoroshiku onegaishimasu."
*How do you do?   *I am pleased to meet you
(lit. I ask for your good favor/help)*

Satomi: "Tomo san, Onaka ga suite imasu ka."

Tomo: "Hai, totemo."
Yes   very

Fumiko wa Tomo ni sandoicchi o

hitotsu agemasu.
1 object

Tomo: "Arigatō gozaimasu. Ā, yokkata!"
Thank you

Tomo wa totemo ureshisō desu.
appears happy

DO YOU UNDERSTAND?

The statements below are all false. Change each one to make it true.

1. Satomi to tomodachi wa kuruma no naka de tabete imasu.

   _____

2. Fumiko wa sandoicchi o mittsu motte imasu. _____

3. Tomo wa resutoran o demasu. _____

4. Tomo wa kanashi sō desu. _____

VERB FOCUS

In English you say "I am _____ " to express how you feel. In Japanese, to express how you feel is "_____ desu". Below are words to express happiness, unhappiness, and all the shades in-between!

ureshī	shiawase	tanoshī	kanashī	mijime	sabishī
happy	*joyful*	*fun*	*sad*	*miserable*	*lonely*

In Japanese there are three different words to express the idea of 'to be'.

IMASU: Animate objects, including humans and animals, but not plants, are paired with this verb to show their location or existence. The particle 'ni' is often used with 'imasu' to express 'at'.

> Example: Satomi to Fumiko wa resutoran ni imasu.
> *Satomi and Fumiko are in a/the restaurant.*

ARIMASU: Show the location, or existence, of inanimate objects. The particle 'ni' is also used with this verb.

> Example: Fujisan wa Nihon ni arimasu.
> *Fuji Mountain is in Japan.*

DESU: This is called a copula, and shows the concept of 'to be' (am, is, are) with nouns, noun phrases, adjectives, etc.

> Examples: Tomo wa totemo genki desu.
> *Tomo is very lively/healthy. (Genki is an adjective.)*

CHAPTER 3

Sumimasen.
Excuse me!/Pardon me!

If you are traveling to a foreign country, there will be many opportunities for you to start a conversation with native speakers of the language. Don't be shy! Of course some people will be in a hurry or won't want to talk to you. However, many people will be interested to meet someone traveling in their country. You'll want to learn some basic questions and appropriate responses as well as some useful expressions. Japanese are very hospitable and interested in travelers from other countries. They will be very *ureshī* to hear you use Japanese!

Nodo ga kawaita/
Kawakimashita
*plain past form/
masu past form
I'm thirsty.
(my throat is dry)*

Tsukareta/Tsukaremashita
*plain past form/masu past form
I'm tired!*

Daijōbu desu.
Don't worry./That's okay.

Gomen nasai.
I'm sorry.

hai	kara	shū	kimasu/kimashita (plain)
yes	*from*	*state*	*come/came*

īe	hanasemasu	irasshaimasu/irasshaimashita (formal)
no	*able to speak*	*come/came (not used when talking about yourself)*

doko/dochira (plain/polite)
where

sukoshi	musuko	musume
a little	*one's own son*	*one's own daughter*

Kochira wa _____ desu.
here is/this is

Watashi no namae wa _____ desu.
my name is

Here are some ways to say yes and no

in Japanese:

HAI!
YES!

ĪE!
NO!

Hai, sō desu.	Ī desu ne.	amari.	zenzen.
Yes, that is so.	*It's good, isn't it.*	*Not much.*	*Not at all. Absolutely not!*

(when used with the negative form)

Sometimes bumping into people by accident can lead to introductions and even friendships. Read what Mr. Dan Newman and Ms. Yoshimi Akagi have to say to each other after they bump into each other in a doorway.

Dan Newman: otoko no hito – *man*   **Yoshimi Akagi:** onna no hito – *woman*
David Newman: otoko no ko – *boy*   **Mari Akagi:** onna no ko – *girl*

1 | **Mr. Newman:** A, sumimasen.   **Ms. Akagi:** Īe. Daijōbu desu yo.
no

2 | **Mr. Newman:** Sumimasen …Ēgo o hanasemasu ka.
Excuse me

Ms. Akagi: Gomen nasai, ēgo wa hanasemasen. Dochira kara irasshaimashita ka.
not able to speak

Mr. Newman: Watashi wa Kororado shū no Denbā kara kimashita. Watashi no
Denver
namae wa Dan Nyūman desu. Hajimemashite.
Newman   How do you do?

Ms. Akagi: Hajimemashite. Watashi no namae wa Akagi Yoshimi desu.
family / first name
Yoroshiku onegai shimasu.
nice to meet you (lit. please treat me kindly)

Mr. Newman: Kochira koso. Dōzo yoroshiku onegai shimasu.
please

3 | **Ms. Akagi:** Watashi no musume o shōkai shimasu. Kore wa Mari desu.
introduce

4 | **Mr. Newman:** Konnichiwa, Mari chan. Oikutsu desu ka.
good afternoon   how old? lit. how many

Mari: Roku sai desu. *(sai = counter for years old)*

5 | **Mr. Newman:** Kore wa watashi no musuko desu. Sukoshi nihongo o hanasemasu.
Japanese

Ms. Akagi: Konnichiwa. Onamae wa nan desu ka.
What is your name?

6 | **David:** Dēbiddo desu. Boku wa nodo ga kawaita.
David

PRACTICE

Study the dialog. Then, see if you can write the missing question. The response is given.

1. _____ ? Roku sai desu.

2. _____ ? Watashi wa Kororado shū kara kimashita.

3. _____ ? Watashi no namae wa Dēbiddo desu.

4. _____ ? Ēgo o hanasemasen.

? ASKING QUESTIONS IN JAPANESE **?**

In Japanese the word *'ka'* indicates a question, acting as a question mark that is verbalized. It is easy to tell if someone is asking you something. However, there are many ways to ask the same question, depending on the formality of the situation. As a guest in Japan you might be addressed in a very formal manner initially, or less formally if Japanese realize you don't understand this honorific language.

Below are some of the most basic questions you will hear in three variations of formality, with the longest generally being the most formal. Responses are also given in order of most formal to least formal. Note that a response will typically omit all the information previously stated or understood. Thus responses are relatively short, even in formal conversation.

Start by memorizing the most formal response as this is always the best and most polite way to address people. Then if you have time, try to memorize the rest. You will certainly hear them while traveling in Japan.

A. What is your name?   Onamae wa nan desu ka.   Risa desu.

Namae wa nan desu ka.   Shōn desu.
                          Sean
* Onamae wa.   Anna desu.

B. Where are you from?   Dochira kara irasshaimashita ka.   Amerika kara kimashita.

Doko kara kimashita ka.   Kankoku kara kimashita.
                           Korea
Dochira kara.   Nyū Yōku kara.
                 New York

C. How old are you?   Oikutsu desu ka.   Roku sai desu.

Nan sai desu ka.   San sai desu.

* Oikutsu.   Kyū sai.

* Although the **desu ka** has been dropped, you will know that it is both polite and a question as the 'O' makes it honorific and the voice will rise slightly at the end, prompting a response from you.

PRACTICE

Now answer the questions below with your own information.

Ex: Dochira kara irasshaimashita ka. Shiatoru kara kimashita. *(I am from Seattle.)*

1.   Oikutsu desu ka. _____ .

2.   Onamae wa. _____ .

3.   Doko kara kimashita ka. _____ .

4.   Nan sai desu ka. _____ .

5.   Namae wa nan desu ka. _____ .

6.   Dochira kara. _____ .

COUNTRIES, LANGUAGES, AND NATIONALITY

In written Japanese (hiragana, katakana, and kanji) there are no spaces between words, capital letters, exclamation points, or question marks. There are commas, periods, and quotation marks. However, when writing in Romaji, spaces are used though typically there are no question marks or exclamation points. Romaji words are capitalized at the head of a sentence and generally for proper names.

What Country	Doko no kuni
USA	Amerika
Japan	Nihon
England	Igirisu
China	Chūgoku
France	Furansu
Germany	Doitsu
Italy	Itaria
Korea	Kankoku
Spain	Supein

Dochira kara irasshaimashita ka. *Amerika* kara desu.

To say the language of a country, simply add "go" to the end of the country name. For example, ***Nihon*** + go = ***Nihongo,*** which is Japanese. ***Chūgoku*** + go = ***Chūgokugo,*** which is Chinese. Easy! English is an exception to the rule you will want to remember. It is not ***Amerikago*** or ***Igirisugo,*** but ***Ēgo.***

'People' or 'person' in Japanese is ***jin.*** Add ***jin*** to the country and you have that person's nationality. A Japanese person is a ***Nihonjin,*** a German is a ***Doitsujin,*** and an American is an ***Amerikajin.***

CHAPTER 4

(O)ikura desu ka.
How much is it?

VOCABULARY

Nani ni nasaimasu ka.
What will you have? (Formal)

Kashikomarimashita.
Certainly. (formal)

Okimari deshō ka.
 Have you made a decision?
(To order/buy)

motto yukkuri
more slowly

Kore o dōzo./ _____ o dōzo.
Here this is./ Here is noun.

HANASU TO WAKARU
to speak   and   to understand

to speak	hanashimasu
to not speak	hanashimasen
can speak	hana<u>se</u>masu
cannot speak	hana<u>se</u>masen
wakarimashita	hanashite kudasai
understood	*please speak*
wakarimasu	wakarimasen
understand	*not understand*

NOTE: With *masu* form verbs *(wakarimasu, hanashimasu, tabemasu)* it is easy to form the negative. Replace the *masu* with *masen.* To form the negative past tense, add *deshita* to *masen.*

Present		Negative		Negative Past
wakarimasu	→	wakarimasen	→	wakarimasen deshita
tabemasu	→	tabemasen	→	tabemasen deshita

You try!

nomimasu (to drink)	not drink _____	did not drink _____
ikimasu (to go)	not go _____	did not go _____

BE POLITE

As you might have noticed in Chapter 3, there are two ways to apologize in Japanese, **sumimasen** and **gomen nasai.** There are also many different ways to say please and thank you. If you can remember just one of each of the phrases for please, thank you and excuse me, your Japanese hosts will be delighted you took the time to learn to "be polite." The golden rule for polite language is that the longer the phrase, the more polite it is! **Dōmo, Dōmo arigatō, Arigatō gozaimasu and Dōmo arigatō gozaimasu** all mean thank you, but can you guess which is the least formal? **'Dōmo'** is the equivalent of a quick 'Thanks' in English.

_____ o kudasai

_____ o onegaishimasu

Dōmo arigatō gozaimasu.
Thank you very much.

Dō itashimashite.
You're welcome.

Kekkō desu.
No thanks.

Sayōnara.
Good bye! (formal, not used among family members)

Jā, mata ne.
See you later. (informal)

STORY

It is 10:00 in the morning. Masako and John are in Tōkyō. Masako is **nihonjin.** Jon is **Amerikajin** but he speaks a little **nihongo.** They are in **panya.**

bakery

Ten-in: Irasshaimase.

Store employee   *Welcome *commonly said when customers enter a restaurant or store.*

Ten-in: Nani ni nasaimasu ka.

Masako: Anpan o kudasai.
sweet bean paste roll

Ten-in: Tsugi no okyakusama, nani ni nasaimasu ka.
next   customer

John: Sumimasen, wakarimasen.

     Motto yukkuri hanashite kudasai.

Ten-in: Hai. Nani ni nasaimasu ka.

John: Kurowassan o futatsu kudasai.
crossaint

Ten-in: Hai, kashikomarimashita.

Masako: Sumimasen, orenji jūsu wa arimasu ka.
orange juice

Ten-in: Hai, kochira desu.
this

Masako: Dōmo. Ikura desu ka.

Ten-in: Ni hyaku en desu.
hundred yen

Masako: Hai, ni hyaku en.

Ten-in: Arigatō gozaimashita.

John and Masako: Dōmo.

WAKARIMASU KA

Do you understand?

Read the previous dialog carefully and see if you can answer these questions in Japanese. Check your answers in the back of the book.

1. Who is **nihonjin** in this dialog? _____

2. Why doesn't John understand? _____

3. What does John want to buy? _____

4. Who asks for orange juice? _____

5. Where does this scene take place? _____

Sūji: jū–ichi – kyū–jū–kyū

Numbers: 11 – 99

Once you know how to count to 10, counting to 99 is easy. Let's start with the numbers from 11 to 19. Say the number for 10, which is **jū**, followed by the next digit:

11	12	13	14	15
jū–ichi	jū–ni	jū–san	jū–yon/shi	jū–go

16	17	18	19
jū–roku	jū–shichi/nana	jū–hachi	jū–kyū/ku

And here's how it works for multiples of 10 and beyond...

20	21	22	30	31	32	40...
ni–jū	ni–jū–ichi	ni–jū–ni	san–jū	san–jū–ichi	san–jū–ni	yon–jū

50...	60...	70...	80...	90...	99...
go–jū	roku–jū	nana–jū	hachi–jū	kyū–ju	kyū–ju–kyū

WHAT WOULD YOU LIKE?

Okimari deshō ka

In the following exercise you are going to order various items, with different shapes and sizes. Flat sheets are counted using *"mai"*. Cups are counted using *"hai"* (or *"bai"* depending on the number). What kind of objects are represented by the counting word *"hon"*?

Write the correct number out in romaji in the blank below and practice saying the phrase, with the appropriate counter word.

1. Hagaki o _____ mai kudasai.
    11

2. Kitte o _____ mai kudasai.
    18

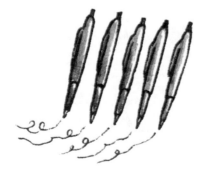

3. Kippu o _____ mai kudasai.
    15

4. Kōhī o _____ bai kudasai.
    3

5. Pen o _____ hon kudasai.
    5

6. Mizu o _____ hon kudasai.
    2

CHAPTER 5

Nan yōbi desu ka
What day is it?

taikutsu
bored, boring

hito me bore
love at first sight

ki ga mijikai
to be quick-tempered

niwa
garden

kaishain
*company employee/
business person*

tanoshī
fun

konpyūta puroguramā
computer programmer

ie
house

kuruma
car

hana
flower

me
eyes

ī
nice

hoshi
star

FOCUS : PARTICLES

Particles are small, but crucial to understanding Japanese grammar and speech. Particles follow the word or phrase that they modify. They can act in many different ways, but below are some of the key particles and their most common uses.

Particle	Definition	Grammatical use	Example
wa	topic marker	Noun1 **wa** noun2 desu.	Jon san wa Amerikajin desu. *Jon is American.*
ga	subject marker	[Topic wa] subject **ga** *(topic can be omitted)*	Yuka san wa shigoto ga suki desu. *Yuki likes work.*
o	direct object marker	Noun **o** verb	Furansupan o tabemasu. *(topic not stated)* *eats French toast*
no	possessive marker	Noun1 **no** noun2	Dēbiddo san no shigoto. *David's job*

to	quotation marker	Person wa "quote" **to** verb	Yuka san "wa konichiwa" to īmashita. *Yuka said "hello."*
	means 'and'	A **to** B	Maikeru san to Yuka san wa Tōkyō ni imasu. *Mike and Yuka are in Tokyo.*
mo	means 'also' or 'too'	Noun **mo**	Jon san wa Amerikajin desu. Dēbiddo san mo Amerikajin desu. *Jon is American.* *David is also American.*
ni de e kara made	indicate direction, relationships or extent		ni *(at/in/toward)* de *(at or by)* e *(towards)* kara *(from)* made *(to)*

NOTE: the order of the subject, topic, and direct object are somewhat flexible as long as the verb is at the end of the sentence.

STORY

Maikeru to Yuka wa ōki na ao to pinku no ie ni sunde imasu. Chīsa na
Michael   big   blue   pink   house in   living   small

niwa ni aka to kīro no hana ga saite imasu.
garden   red   yellow   flower   blooming

Maikeru wa konpyūtā puroguramā desu. Ni-jū-go sai de, me ga midori desu.
green

Totemo ī hito desu ga, sukoshi ki ga mijikai desu. Maikeru wa shigoto ga suki de
work/job   like

wa arimasen. Maikeru no shigoto wa taikutsu desu.
neg. of desu=not

Maikeru wa Yuka ni hito me bore shimashita. Yuka wa kaishain desu.

Ni-jū-roku sai de, me ga chairo desu. Tanoshī hito desu. Yuka no shigoto wa
brown

omoshiroi desu. Yuka wa shigoto ga totemo suki desu. Futari tomo totemo isogashī desu.
interesting   both of them   busy

Yuka wa maishū getsu-yōbi ni,
every week   Monday

densha de Ōsaka ni ikimasu.
train   by   go

Maikeru wa maishū sui-yōbi ni
Wednesday

kuruma de Yokohama ni ikimasu.

Demo, maishū kin-yōbi wa futari de "Akaboshi"
Friday   two people   Red Star

to iu resutoran de shokuji o shimasu.
called   meal   have/do.

PRACTICE

Complete the following sentences in Japanese. Use the vocabulary and the dialog to help you.

1. Michael and Yuka live in a big blue and pink _____.

2. Michael is 25 _____.

3. Generally, Michael is very _____.

4. Yuka is _____.

5. Michael doesn't like his _____.

6. Yuka goes to Ōsaka by _____.

7. Michael goes to Yokohama by _____.

shiro

ao

gurē

chairo

kuro

orenji

kīro

midori

pinku

aka

IRO
color

Use the clues in English to find the word in nihongo. Hint: If the word has an extended vowel you need to write it twice in the puzzle (e.g. kōcha = koocha)

ACROSS

2. black
6. green
8. white
9. grey

DOWN

1. red
3. orange
4. brown
5. blue
7. pink

DAYS OF THE WEEK

Nan yōbi desu ka

Days of the week in Japanese are named after the elements and planets. As in English, the first part of each word has a different meaning, but they all end in *yōbi* (day). The Kanji for Sunday, *nichi,* means sun, just as it does in English. See if you can notice any other similar origins in meaning! *Getsu* means moon, *ka* is fire, *sui* represents water, *moku* is wood, *kin* is gold, and *do* means earth.

Nichi-yōbi	Getsu-yōbi	Ka-yōbi	Sui-yōbi	Moku-yōbi	Kin-yōbi	Do-yōbi
Sunday	*Monday*	*Tuesday*	*Wednesday*	*Thursday*	*Friday*	*Saturday*

Find the Japanese days of the week hidden in the puzzle. Then circle them. Two are missing.

w	c	n	x	w	i	y	g	n	g
h	g	i	m	d	o	e	o	q	l
m	r	c	s	o	t	o	l	m	s
r	v	h	e	s	n	w	d	u	t
n	e	i	u	o	q	n	i	k	t
n	g	t	o	v	u	t	w	c	z
k	u	m	a	p	k	f	i	r	e
d	a	s	a	w	o	d	x	z	k
m	q	t	p	o	m	k	m	k	e
h	t	r	a	e	s	i	y	b	f

PRACTICE

Put the *(yōbi)* in their correct order by putting a number from 1–7 in front of each day.
NOTE: In Japan the week is considered to begin with Sunday!

_____ sui-yōbi   _____ nichi-yōbi   _____ ka-yōbi   _____ kin-yōbi

_____ getsu-yōbi   _____ do-yōbi   _____ moku-yōbi

CHAPTER 6

Tōi desu ka.
Is it far?

Understanding directions in another language is particularly difficult, but not impossible! Of course it helps to have a map so you can look at the names of the streets as the person you ask points to them. You don't have to understand every word.

shimatte imasu
to be closed

tōi
far

aite imasu
to be open

chikai
near

sanpo shimasu
take a walk

watarimasu
cross

LISTEN FOR THE VERB.
This will generally be the first word you hear because it will be in the command form: *aruite, notte, itte, magatte, agatte, orite, watatte.*

LISTEN FOR THE DIRECTION WORDS.
tonari ni, ni men shite

LISTEN FOR THE NAMES OF THE STREETS.
These will be the hardest to understand. (You can learn verbs and directions in advance, but names of people and places are more difficult because they may sound unfamiliar to a visitor.)

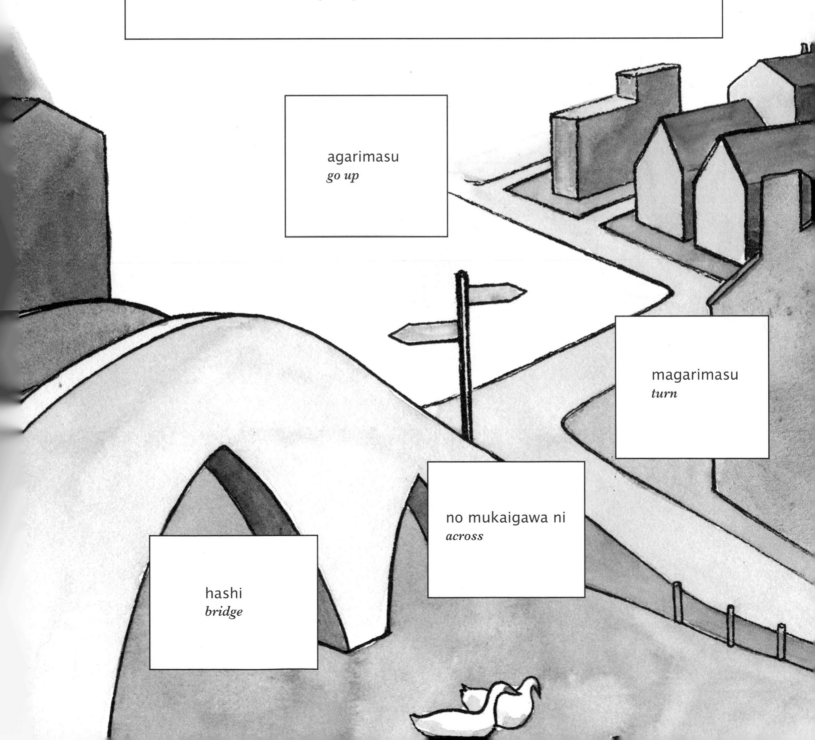

agarimasu
go up

magarimasu
turn

no mukaigawa ni
across

hashi
bridge

DIRECTIONS

hantaigawa ni
on the other side

tonari ni
next to, beside

ni men shite
facing

tsukiatarimasu
dead end

hidari ni
to the left

massugu
straight ahead

migi ni
to the right

VERBS USED WHEN GIVING DIRECTIONS

Infinitive (plain form)	Definition	Polite form	Command form *add **kudasai** (please) for politeness
aruku	*to walk*	arukimasu	aruite (kudasai)
noru	*to ride*	norimasu	notte (kudasai)
iku	*to go*	ikimasu	itte (kudasai)
magaru	*to turn*	magarimasu	magatte (kudasai)
agaru	*to go up*	agarimasu	agatte (kudasai)
oriru	*to go down*	orimasu	orite (kudasai)
wataru	*to cross*	watarimasu	watatte (kudasai)
hairu	*to enter*	hairimasu	haitte (kudasai)

ORDINAL NUMBERS

The counter for ordinal numbers is **ban.** Ordinal numbers will also be useful in order to understand directions (e.g. turn right at the first street).

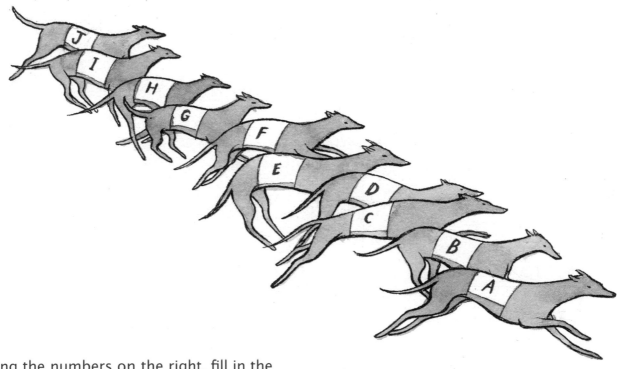

Using the numbers on the right, fill in the blanks to help the race announcer list the winner and the first nine runner–ups. Say each number as you write it.

*Add **me** to **ichiban** or another ordinal number and it indicates that number in a series.

A is _____	F is _____	ichiban	1st	rokuban	6th
B is _____	G is _____	niban	2nd	nanaban	7th
C is _____	H is _____	sanban	3rd	hachiban	8th
D is _____	I is _____	yonban	4th	kyūban	9th
E is _____	J is _____	goban	5th	jūban	10th

DIALOG

Mr. Kanda and Ms. Hattori are standing outside a hotel, talking.

Ms. Hattori: Kanda san, kyō wa doko ni ikimasu ka.
today

Mr. Kanda: Mazu ginkō ni ikimasu. Sorekara depāto de
first
kaimono o shimasu. Hattori san wa.
shopping

Ms. Hattori: Watashi wa ēga ni ikitai desu.
movie   want to go

Mr. Kanda: Demo kyō wa ka-yōbi deshō. Ēgakan wa aite imasen yo.
movie theater   not open

Ms. Hattori: Sō desu ne. Zannen. Jā, hakubutsukan ni ikitai desu.
too bad   museum

Mr. Kanda: Tōkyō kokuritsu hakubutsukan wa dō desu ka. Ka-yōbi ni aite imasu yo.
Tokyo National Museum   open

Ms. Hattori: Ī desu ne. Tōkyō Kokuritsu Hakubutsukan wa doko desu ka. Tōi desu ka.

Mr. Kanda: Īe, amari tōkunai desu. Aruite, nijūgo fun gurai desu. Kono michi o
not far   minutes about

massugu itte, ichiban me no tōri o hidari ni magarimasu.
first
Kototoi dōri desu. Kototoi dōri o massugu ikuto, migi gawa ni

hakubutsukan ga arimasu.

Ms. Hattori: Wakarimashita. Kototoi dōri o massugu ikuto, hakubutsukan ga migi gawa ni

arimasu ne.

Mr. Kanda: Sō desu.

Ms. Hattori: Arigatō gozaimasu. Sore ja, itte kimasu.
*Well then,   *lit. "I'll go and come" - a set phrase said when leaving
the house (or in this case hotel)*

Mr. Kanda: Hai, ki o tsukete, itte rasshai
*take care   *lit. "Go and come back" - set response to "Itte kimasu."*

WAKARIMASU KA

Do you understand?

Answer **hai** or **īe.**

1. Ēgakan wa ka- yōbi ni aite imasu. _____

2. Tōkyō Kokuritsu Hakubutsukan wa kyō aite imasu. _____

3. Hattori san wa ginkō ni ikimasu ka. _____

4. Tōkyō Kokuritsu Hakubutsukan wa tōi desu ka. _____

CHAPTER 7

Dono kisetsu ga suki desu ka.
Which season do you like?

tokidoki
sometimes

suki (na) + noun
to like something

hanami
cherry blossom viewing in spring

THE SEASONS OF THE YEAR

Japanese are wonderfully aware of the seasons and will often comment proudly that Japan is a land of four **kisetsu,** or **shiki** (literally 4 seasons). Not only does the weather radically change, the food, celebrations, color schemes, and other symbols are also seasonal. Winter is dominated by the New Year celebration, when Japanese clean their homes, visit shrines for good luck, and spend time with their families. Spring is cherry blossom season and the beginning of the fiscal and school year. Summer is a good time to see summer festivals that might include traditional dancing, fireworks, and women dressed in Yukata (cotton kimonos). In the fall, the foliage is a highlight as well as Sports and Culture Day Events held in each town and village.

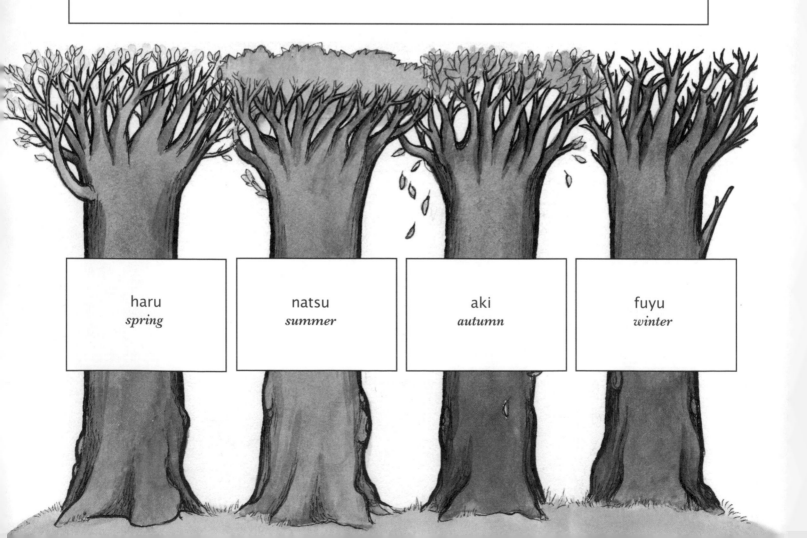

haru
spring

natsu
summer

aki
autumn

fuyu
winter

THE MONTHS OF THE YEAR

Tsuki

Tsuki, month, also means moon. The pronunciation, or reading of the Chinese character moon changes depending on how (or with what) it is used. As the heavenly body, it is *tsuki,* but in Monday (moon day) it is *getsu,* and in the months of the year it is pronounced *gatsu.* But from there it's easy, just count from 1–12 (beginning with January) and add *gatsu.*

ichi-gatsu
January

ni-gatsu
February

san-gatsu
March

shi-gatsu
April

go-gatsu
May

roku-gatsu
June

shichi-gatsu
July

hachi-gatsu
August

ku-gatsu
September

jū-gatsu
October

jū-ichi-gatsu
November

jū-ni-gatsu
December

STORY

Look at the pictures and read the sentences under each one. See if you can figure out the *imi* (meaning). Write what you think the sentences mean in the blanks. Use the vocabulary and idioms on the previous pages to help you **wakarimasu** the story that follows the pictures.

haha	**chichi**	**imōto**	**otōto**	**ani**	**ane**
my mother (familiar)	*my father*	*my younger sister*	*my younger brother*	*my older brother*	*my older sister*

Haha wa natsu ni umi ni ikimasu.
      ocean

1. _____

Chichi wa fuyu ni yama ni ikimasu.
    mountain

2. _____

Otōto wa aki ni haikingu o shimasu.
    hiking

3. _____

Imōto to watashi wa haru ni hana o tsumimasu.
     flower   *to pick*

4. _____

Watashi no namae wa Airīn Hanson desu. Ni-jū-ni sai desu. Watashi no kazoku wa totemo
22 years old   *family*

omoshiroi desu. Minna suki na koto ga chigaimasu.
       Everyone   *thing*   *to be different*

Haha wa natsu ga suki desu. Natsu ni umi ni ikimasu. Chichi wa fuyu ga suki desu. Fuyu

ni yama ni ikimasu. Sukī ga daisuki desu. Otōto no Sukotto wa jū-nana sai de, haikingu ga
     skiing   *to like very much*   *Scott*

suki desu. Ku-gatsu to jū-gatsu ni yama ni ikimasu. Imōto no Arisu wa jū-go sai de,
                                         Alice

haru ga ichiban suki desu. Watashi mo haru ga ichiban suki desu. Watashi to Arisu wa
favorite/like most

haru ni hanami o shimasu. Watashi wa san-gatsu to shi-gatsu no ryokō ga suki desu ga,
                                       a trip   *but*

Arisu wa amari ryokō ga suki de wa arimasen. Sate, watashitachi wa itsu minna de
                       well then   *when*   *with everyone*

dekakeru no deshō ka. Jitsu wa ichinenjū desu. Ku-gatsu ni haikingu ni ikimasu.
to go out (plain form)   *the truth is*   *year round*

Tokidoki fuyu to haru ni mo haikingu ni ikimasu. Jū-ni-gatsu kara san-gatsu made wa
                                    from   *to*

sukī ni ikimasu. Roku-gatsu to shichi-gatsu to hachi-gatsu ni wa yoku umi ni ikimasu.

Mochiron, tokidoki ie ni mo imasu. Sorede minna shiawase desu.
of course   *that way/therefore*   *happy*

PRACTICE

A. See if you can translate the following sentences into English.

1. Chichi wa fuyu ga suki desu.

_____.

2. Otōto no Sukotto wa haikingu ga suki desu.

_____.

3. Watashi no kazoku wa itsu ryokō ni ikimasu ka.

_____.

4. Tokidoki fuyu to haru ni mo haikingu ni ikimasu.

_____.

B.   Now try to translate these sentences into Japanese.

1. I'm 22 years old.

_____.

2. My younger brother likes the mountains.

_____.

3. I also like spring the most!

_____.

4. In June, July, and August (we) go to the ocean.

_____.

LOAN WORDS

sumāto
trim/fashionable

sarariman
business man

Japanese have a long history of borrowing words from other cultures. The largest number of borrowed words come from Chinese, adopted in the 5th century along with Chinese Kanji. More recently, the majority of adopted words come from English, although there are also German, Portugese, Italian, and Dutch loan words. The woman above looks *'sumāto'* meaning trim and fashionable, not intelligent. The man is a *'sararīman',* or typical Japanese business man.

You can see that often the original meaning has been altered or changed to become uniquely Japanese. Try to match the words in the box with a picture and their meaning. Hint: The picture may represent part of the loan word **or** be a clue to its meaning.

1. _____ girl

2. _____ beach

3. _____ family doctor

4. _____ cheese

5. _____ car navigation system

6. _____ boyfriend

7. _____ wake-up call

8. _____ off-season

9. _____ apartment building

10. _____ new-release movie

A.	shīzun ofu	F.	bīchi
B.	bōifurendo	G.	famirī dokutā
C.	kā-nabi	H.	mōningu kōru
D.	manshon	I.	gāru
E.	rōdo shō	J.	chīzu

CHAPTER 8

Kochira wa tonari no Suzuki san no gokazoku desu.
This is my neighbor Suzuki's family.

There is a good chance that if you stay in Japan you will get to know your neighbors. In Chapter 7 you learned how to talk about your own family or people close to you. This chapter introduces the honorific forms and vocabulary used to talk about others.

bōshi
hat

megane
glasses

(se ga) takai
(height) tall

kami no ke
hair

nagai
long

(se ga) hikui
(height) short

goshujin
husband (not your own spouse)

okusan
wife (not your own spouse)

Gokazoku
family-honorific

MALE

otōsan
father

ojīsan
grandfather

giri no otōsan
father-in-law

musukosan
son

onīsan
older brother

otōtosan
younger brother

ojisan
uncle

oigosan
nephew

NOTE: Notice how many of the following words end in **'san'** and begin in **'O'** or **'Go'**. These prefixes and suffixes are added to make the words honorific, or polite. Often these are dropped, making the word still polite but not quite as honorific. You have already learned a few of these honorific phrases such as: **Ohisashiburi** (Long time no see) and **Oikura** (how much)

FEMALE

okāsan
mother

obāsan
grandmother

giri no okāsan
mother-in-law

musumesan
daughter

onēsan
older sister

imōtosan
younger sister

obasan
aunt

mēgosan
niece

STORY

Suzuki san no gokazoku wa suteki na gokazoku desu.   Okāsan no
nice   *mother*

onamae wa Nobuko san desu. Nobuko san wa kami no ke ga gurē de, mijikai

desu. Totemo genki na hito desu. Otōsan no onamae wa Yoshihisa san desu.
father

Yoshihisa san wa yoku bōshi o kaburimasu. Se ga takai desu. Suzuki san wa
wear

onīsan ga hitori imasu. Onīsan no onamae wa Hiroshi san desu. Hiroshi san wa totemo
older brother   one person

tanoshī hito de, Suzuki san no okusan no onēsan no Shinko san to kekkon shite imasu.
is married

Shinko san wa totemo kirē desu. Kami no ke ga nagai desu. Totemo
pretty

yasashī hito desu. Kodomo san wa imasen. Suzuki san no giri no okāsan to giri no
children/child   *mother-in-law*

otōsan no onamae wa Yamauchi Mayumi san to Yamauchi Kenichirō san desu. Suzuki
father-in-law

san no okusan no onamae wa Rie san desu. Rie san wa se ga hikui desu. Atama ga ī

desu. Musume san ga hitori imasu. Musume san no onamae wa Saori san desu. Saori san

wa jū–san sai desu. Saori san wa supōtsu ga suki de, genki ippai desu.
full of energy

Suzuki san wa totemo hansamu desu.
handsome

Fill in the blanks under each picture.

a) Write the name of the person.
b) Write what relationship that person is to Mr. Suzuki.

1. a _____
   b _____
2. a _____
   b _____

3. a _____
   b _____
4. a _____
   b _____

(Mr. Suzuki)

5. a _____
   b _____

6. a _____
   b _____
7. a _____
   b _____

8. a _____
   b _____

FOCUS

Japanese adjectives modify a noun, but they come in more shapes and forms than English adjectives. Japanese adjectives can be used directly before a noun or after a noun with a subject marker. There are 2 basic groups of adjectives: *'i'* adjectives and *'na'* adjectives.

'I' Adjectives:

Note they always end with an 'i'* Ex.: ***takai, mijikai, muzukashī*** (difficult)

BEFORE A NOUN:	THE NEGATIVE:
se ga takai hito *a tall person*	Drop the final 'i' and add 'kunai' takai: taka + kunai = takakunai
AFTER A NOUN:	mijikai: mijika + kunai = mijikakunai
Watashi wa se ga takai desu. *I am tall.*	muzukashī: muzukashi + kunai = muzukashikunai

*Be careful; you cannot automatically assume all adjectives that end in *'i'* are *'i'* adjectives. For example, ***kirai*** (dislike/hate) is a *'na'* adjective.

GIVE IT A TRY!

Try forming the negative forms of:

kuroi *(black)* nagai *(long)* hosoi *(thin/narrow)*

_____ _____ _____

'Na' Adjectives:

Act grammatically like nouns. Some ***na*** adjectives that have been introduced are ***kirē na*** (pretty), ***hansamu na*** (handsome), ***suki na*** (like), and ***kirai na*** (hate/dislike).

BEFORE A NOUN: noun + na kirē na hito *a pretty person*	THE NEGATIVE: Use a negative verb… kirē desu → kirē de wa arimasen (polite) → kirē de wa nai (plain)
AFTER A NOUN: drop 'na' and use a verb or copula (such as desu) Ano hito wa kirē desu. *That person is pretty.*	…or to modify a noun in the negative… kirē na hito → kirē de wa nai hito

NOTE: In Japanese there are two groups of words to refer to family. One set is honorific and would be used when talking about the families of others or when addressing your own older family members. The other set is familiar, and less honorific, and is used when talking about your own family to others. Just as you wouldn't refer to yourself with the honorific, *'san'*, you also don't want to elevate your own family when talking to others. In chapter 7, terms to describe your immediate family were introduced and in this chapter terms to describe another's family were introduced. A few other 'familiar' terms you might want to know are:

haha	chichi	ane	ani
my mother	*my father*	*my older sister*	*my older brother*

oya	imōto	otōto
my parent (s)	*my younger sister*	*my younger brother*

shujin, otto	kanai, tsuma
my husband	*my wife*

PRACTICE

Write the sentences below in Japanese, practice using the adjective before and after the subject.

The first two are done for you.

1. *(tall) mother*   se ga takai okāsan

2. *(pretty) daughter*   kirē na musumesan

3. *(fun) husband*   _____

4. *grandmother (interesting)*   _____

5. *haikingu (not like)*   _____

6. *(handsome) uncle*   _____

CHAPTER 9

Samusugimasu.
It's too cold!

Being able to chat about **tenki** (the weather) is a useful skill to have in another language. Whether you're at a bus stop, or making small talk with a desk clerk at a hotel, **tenki** is a safe and popular topic (and often necessary if you're planning outdoor activities).

NOTE: The subject of the sentence is usually inferred. **Atsui desu** could mean It is hot or I am hot. **Watashi wa atsui desu** would clarify that I am hot. Words to describe weather are generally **ī** adjectives and nouns. The four **ī** adjectives below are **atsui, samui, ī,** and **warui.** The nouns, **ame, yuki, kaze and hare** act grammatically like **na** adjectives, except you connect them to another word using **no. "Ame no hi"** means a "rainy day" or literally, a day of rain. Review chapter 8 if you have forgotten how to use adjectives.

atsui
hot

samui
cold

kaze
wind

ame
rain

hare
sunny/clear

ī tenki/ tenki ga ī
fine weather

warui tenki /
tenki ga warui
bad weather

yuki
snow

This is a telephone conversation between *Makiko to Makiko no okāsan. Makiko wa ni-jū-ni sai* and is living in Alaska for 1 year doing research as part of her university graduate studies. *Makiko no okāsan* lives in *Fukuoka.*

NOTE: This is an example of female speech in plain/informal style. This is the common level of speech used among family members. In this informal style, sentences often end with *wa* (as an assertion or to soften the meaning), *yo* (assertion), and *no* (question or statement).

Makiko: Moshi, moshi. Maki desu.
Hello (only used on the telephone)

Okāsan: A, Maki chan. Genki.

Makiko: Genki da kedo samui wa.

Okāsan: Taihen ne. Yuki aru no.
That's too bad.

Makiko: Okāsan. Arasuka no fuyu yo. Mochiron,
                                         of course

yuki ippai aru wa yo.

Fukuoka no tenki wa dō.

Okāsan: Kyō wa ame da kedo, kinō wa hare datta wa. Kyō wa Samui wa. Mata ashita
                                                                   tomorrow

wa hare da sō yo. Maki chan, itsu kaeru no.
I hear   apparently   kaerimasu/return

Makiko: Wakaranai wa. Ima shigoto ga isogashī no.
                                           now

Nichi-yōbi igai wa mainichi shigoto yo.
                      except   everyday

Okāsan: Sō, taihen ne. Doko de shigoto o shiteru no.
suru=to do

Makiko: Maishū Nōmu ni shucchō suru no.
Nome   business trip

Hikōki de iku no yo.
plane

Feabankusu ni mo yoku iku no. Kuruma de iku kedo
Fairbanks

koko kara tōi no yo. Ankarejji de shigoto o suru hō ga
Anchorage

suki. Okāsan wa itsu asobi ni kuru no.
come for fun / to hang out (lit. come play)

Okāsan: Ima wa hidoi kisetsu ja nai no. Fuyu de
terrible   isn't it?

wa nai hō ga ī wa. Okāsan wa yuki ga kirai na no.

Natsu ni Arasuka ni ikitai wa.

Makiko: Sō ne. Arasuka no fuyu wa

samui wa. Watashi wa kondo fuyu yasumi
next winter vacation

ni Nihon ni kaeritai wa.
want to return

Okāsan: Ī wa ne. Hayaku kaette kite.
come back soon

Koko wa itsumo ī tenki yo.

Makiko: Sō. Jā, mata denwa suru wa.
to call/phone

Okāsan: Hai, matteru wa. Ganbatte ne.
I'll be waiting

PRACTICE

Wakarimasu ka.
Do you understand?

See if you can answer the following questions based on the dialog.

1. Dare ga samui desu ka. _____

2. Makiko wa doko desu ka. _____

3. Doko de ame deshita ka. _____

4. Makiko wa itsu shigoto o shimasu ka. _____

5. Okāsan wa itsu Arasuka ni ikitai desu ka. _____

See if you can match each statement on the right to the appropriate picture of the person to make each statement true. Connect each of the circles with a line.

① "Ame yo" to īmasu.

② Samui desu.

③ Getsu-yōbi kara doyōbi made shigoto.

④ "Yuki ga kirai na no." to īmasu.

⑤ Hikōki to kuruma de shucchō ni ikimasu.

⑥ Natsu ni Arasuka ni ikitai desu.

⑦ Fuyu yasumi ni nihon ni kaerimasu.

⑧ Ankarejji de shigoto o suru hō ga suki desu.

PRACTICE

Nihon no tenki wa dō desu ka.
How is the weather in Japan?

Let's see if you can complete the sentences with the weather expressions given. (You can peak back at Chapter 7 to review *tsuki* and *kisetsu*)

1. Natsu wa
   _____.
   it is hot

2. Roku-gatsu wa
   _____.
   it is rainy (rain)

3. Jū-gatsu wa
   _____.
   it's good weather

4. Ichi-gatsu wa
   _____.
   it snows

5. Haru wa
   _____.
   it is windy

6. Kyō wa
   _____.
   it's bad weather

EXPRESSIONS FOR TIME

To talk about the weather, or the weather forecast, time words like yesterday, today, and tomorrow will be useful.

senshū
last week

ototoi
the day before yesterday

raishū
next week

asatte
the day after tomorrow

kinō
yesterday

kyō
today

ashita
tomorrow

VERB CONJUGATIONS

going, coming, and returning

Iku: to go

iki+ mashita	*went*
iki + mashō	*let's go*
Itte kudasai	*please go*

Kuru: to come

ki + mashita	*came*
ki+te+kudasai	*please come*
verb stem + ni + kimasu	*come and do + verb*
	(asobi ni kimasu come and play/spend time relaxing.)

Kaeru: to return

kaeri + mashita	*returned/ went home*
kaeri + mashō	*let's return/let's go home*
kaeri+tai	*want to go home*
o kaeri + nasai	*welcome back*
	* set phrase said to
	the one returning home

These directional verbs need particles to show where the person is going to or from, and occasionally by what means they are travelling. The most common particles used with directional verbs are:

ni/e/made	*to/towards*
kara	*from*
de	*by (mode of transportion)*

Remember that the particle comes after the noun or phrase it modifies.

Hikōki de nihon ni kaerimasu.
Plane by Japan to return.   (I) return to Japan by airplane.

Nihon kara Arasuka made ikimasu.
Japan from Alaska to go.   (I) go from Japan to Alaska.

See if you can figure out which word doesn't belong in each of the series of words below. Write the words in the blanks.

_____	1.	atsui	natsu	hare	samui
_____	2.	kinō	samui	ashita	asatte
_____	3.	takusan	itsu	doko	dare
_____	4.	ikimasu	kimasu	kochira	kaerimasu
_____	5.	gatsu	shū	nen	haru

CHAPTER 10

Nan ji desu ka.
What time is it?

You've learned **nan yōbi** (Chapter 5) and **nan gatsu** (Chapter 7). Now it's time to learn about how to tell time. If you need to, go back to Chapters 2 and 4 to review the numbers. Later in this chapter you'll learn some more numbers that you'll need in order to say the minutes.

kigen ga ī/ gokigen
to be in a good mood

kigen ga warui
to be in a bad mood

hayai
to be early or fast

osoi
to be late or slow

eki
railroad station

kippu
ticket/tickets

noriba
track

DIALOG

Shigenobu to Hanayo wa Ōsaka eki ni imasu. Densha de Kinosaki no
                                              train

tomodachi no ie ni asobi ni ikimasu.

Shigenobu: Sumimasen, tsugi no Kinosaki yuki no densha wa nan ji desu ka.
                        next   *heading to*

Eki – In: Tsugi wa jū ji jū-kyū fun desu.
(station employee)   *10:19*

Shigenobu: Sumimasen, mō ichi do
                        again
    onegaishimasu.

Eki – In: Jū ji jū-kyū fun desu.

Shigenobu: Ima nan ji desu ka.
    now

Eki – In: Jū ji jū-ro ppun desu.   Ato san pun desu yo.
                        10:16   *after 3 min.*

Shigenobu: Ato san pun!

Hanayo: Shimatta. Maniaimasen ne.
    Darn!   *(maniau) not make it/not be on time*

Shigenobu: Mata. Watashitachi itsumo osoi desu ne.
    again   *always*

Hanayo: Shigenobu san, kyō wa kigen ga warui desu ne.

Shigenobu: Yamete kudasai.
    please stop/stop it!

59

Hanayo: Sono tsugi no Kinosaki yuki wa nan ji desu ka.
Eki-in ni   *the next*   *heading to*   *the next*

Eki – In: Ēto….. Jū–san ji yon–jū–nana fun desu.
      let's see   *13:47*

Kyūkō desu ga.
express train but

Hanayo: Jā, ni mai kudasai.
Eki-in ni

Eki – In: Katamichi desu ka. Ōfuku desu ka.
      one-way   *round-trip*

Hanayo: Ōfuku kippu kudasai.

Eki – In: Hai, ichi–man en desu.
        10,000 yen

Hanayo: Dōmo. Nanban noriba desu ka.
        what number

Eki – In: Hachiban desu.
      number 8

Shigenobu: Jā, nanika nomimasen ka.
Hanayo ni   *why don't we drink something?*

Hanayo: Ī desu yo.

Shigenobu: Yokatta. Ikimashō.

DO YOU UNDERSTAND?

Answer True or False to the following statements based on the dialog.

_____ 1. Shigenobu san to Hanayo san wa hikōki de ikimasu.

_____ 2. Shigenobu san wa "Ima nan ji desu ka." to kikimasu.

_____ 3. "Hanayo san wa kigen ga warui desu ne." to Shigenobu ga īmasu.

_____ 4. Hanayo san wa densha no kippu o san mai kaimasu.

to buy

_____ 5. Ōfuku kippu o kaimasu.

TELLING TIME

Expressing time in Japanese is easy. You need to be able to count to 12 to say the hours and to 60 to say the minutes. Or you can just say **goro** (about) and avoid saying the exact minute. Usually Japanese specify the time of day, such as **asa no** or **hiru no** when using the 12-hour clock to avoid ambiguity, unless it is clear from the context. Japanese also often use **gozen** (before noon=am) and **gogo** (after noon=pm) before the number to be absolutely clear.

In Japan, the 24-hour system of telling time ('military time' as we call it in the U.S.) is usually used on TV and radio, with travel schedules, appointments, and theater and concert times in order to avoid ambiguity. Just subtract 12 to figure out the time.

shichi ji   jyū-ni ji   san ji   hachi ji

asa no...   shōgo   hiru no...   yoru no...
in the morning   *noon*   *in the afternoon*   *in the evening*

Here are the ways to add the minutes when you are telling time:

 Asa no
Jū–ichi ji yon–ju ppun

 Gozen
shichi ji ni–ju ppun

 Gogo
ni ji go–ju ppun

 Asa no
ku–ji san–ju ppun

You will be learning how to count over 100, which is very systematic and easy!

To tell the time you:

hour + **"ji"** + minute + **"pun/fun"**

The tricky part is knowing when to add **"fun"** or **"pun"**.

Pun is used with numbers ending in 1, 3, 6, 8, and 0; and they change sounds (except 3).

Fun is used with numbers ending in 2, 4, 5 and 9. These numbers do not change their sound.

PRACTICE
Nan ji desu ka?

Match the times with the clocks. Write the correct letter under each clock.

a. Jū ji jū go fun desu.   c. Jūichi ji sanjūhappun desu.   e. Ku ji yonjūnana fun desu.
b. Yo ji yonjūgofun desu. d. Go ji han desu.

1. _____   2. _____   3. _____   4. _____   5. _____

Sūji Counting to 100

You already have had some practice with all the numbers you need to tell time. Let's review and see how much you remember. Read the pronunciation carefully and say each number out loud.

Since a vending machine beverage costs 150 yen, to really shop in Japan you need to know the higher counting unites of **sen** (1000), **man** (10,000), or for big spenders, **oku** (100,000,000). The symbol ¥ represents the Japanese currency and is pronounced 'en'. Dinner might cost **ni sen en** (¥2,000), **san man en** (¥30,000) could easily be the cost of a fine hotel, while the entire visit could be as little as **jū man en** (¥100,000) or as much as **hyaku man en** (¥1,000,000). I hope you never get a bill for **go oku en** (¥500,000,000)!

23	二十三	ni-jū-san		40	四十	yon-jū
24	二十四	ni-jū-yon		50	五十	go-jū
25	二十五	ni-jū-go		60	六十	roku-jū
26	二十六	ni-jū-roku		70	七十	nana-jū
27	二十七	ni-jū-nana		71	七十一	nana-jū-ichi
28	二十八	ni-jū-hachi		72	七十二	nana-jū-ni
29	二十九	ni-jū-kyū		80	八十	hachi-jū
30	三十	san-jū		90	九十	kyū-jū
31	三十一	san-jū-ichi		95	九十五	kyū-jū-go
32	三十二	san-jū-ni		100	百	hyaku

DOUBLE TROUBLE:

In Japanese there are many words that sound the same but have very different meanings. In the written language, their meaning is usually clear due to their kanji. In the spoken language sometimes the pitch, or tone, of one word will distinguish it from the other. As a beginner, you will usually depend on context to help clarify the meaning.

Some examples:

Ame: rain (雨), candy (あめ)   Sake: rice wine (酒), salmon (鮭)

Hashi: bridge (橋), chopsticks (箸)   Kami: paper (紙), hair (髪), god (神)

Kaki: parsimmon (柿), oyster (カキ)

CHAPTER 11

Hima na toki, nani o shimasu ka.
What do you do in your free time?

pika pika
sparkling clean

asa ichiban ni
at the crack of dawn/first one up

ryōri ga tokui
be good at cooking

FOCUS: PREPOSITIONS

ni
in

no mae
in front of

no shita
under

no naka
inside

no ue
on

no ushiro
behind

no soto
outside

no yoko
next to

USEFUL EXPRESSIONS

wakai
young (not used for children)

webusaito o mimasu
surf the Web

ī–mēru o kakimasu
write email

VOCABULARY

ikkai
first floor/downstairs

ni kai
2nd floor/upstairs

inu
dog

hito
human(s)

chīsai
small (also means 'young' for children)

konpūta
computer

neko
cat

nenpai
old/elderly (only for people)

STORY

Chibi wa kawaī chairo no inu desu. Kuro neko no Kiki to issho ni
cute   *black cat*

sunde imasu. Sono ie ni hito ga san nin imasu: onna no hito to nenpai no otoko no hito
3 people

to chīsai otoko no ko desu. Sono ie wa itsumo pika pika de kimochi ga ī desu.
has a good feeling

Chibi wa yoku ni kai no Daiki no shinshitsu
bedroom

made asobi ni ikimasu. Daiki wa nana sai desu.

Daiki ga omocha de asonde iru toki, Chibi wa beddo
toy   *while playing*   *bed*

no ue ni suwarimasu. Kiki wa beddo no shita de nemasu.
on top of   to sit   *under   sleep*

Daiki no ojīsan no Gentarō wa ryōri ga tokui desu.

Chibi wa daidokoro no sutobu no yoko
kitchen   stove   next to

ni suwaru no ga suki desu. Kiki wa mado no mae de nemasu.
suwarimasu   *window   in front of*

Chibi wa asa nebō o suru no ga suki desu ga,
sleep in late   to do (shimasu)

Daiki no okāsan no Yukari wa, asa ichi ban ni

Konpyūta o tsukemasu. Soshite, ofisu de
turn on   office

ī-mēru o kaitari, iron na webusaito o mitari shimasu.
kakimasu

Kiki wa gomibako no naka de nemasu.
garbage can   inside of

Hima na toki, Yukari wa hon o yomu no ga suki desu. Daiki wa piano o hiku no ga suki
free time   book   read   to play an instrament (hikimasu)

desu. Daiki ga piano o hiku to, Chibi wa sofa no ushiro ni kakuremasu. Kiki wa piano no oto
sofa   behind   to hide (kakureu)   sound/noise

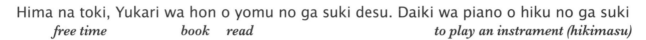

ga suki de wa nai no de, soto de nemasu.
because outside

Kin-yōbi no yoru, Gentarō to Yukari to Daiki wa

taitē ni kai no ima de terebi o mitari, toranpu
usually   to watch TV   play cards

o shitari, hon o yondari shimasu.
read books (yomimaus)

Kiki wa isu de nete, Chibi wa kazoku no yoko ni suwarimasu.
chair   to sleep (neru)

WAKARIMASU KA

Nani ga suki desu ka (What do they like?) Match the members of the family with the things they like to do. Write the letters in the blanks.

1. Chibi wa _____

2. Kiki wa _____

3. Yukari wa _____

4. Gentarō wa _____

5. Daiki wa _____

A.

B.

C.

D.

E.

In Japanese you can't link a verb and a noun or noun phrase like **'suki desu'** (like) directly. **'Sakkā o shimasu suki desu',** is difficult to understand and grammatically incorrect. To say you like to do an activity, link the verb and noun phrases together by doing the following:

Plain form of verb + **no ga** + **suki desu** = like to <u>verb</u>

Write the letter of the matching Japanese sentences next to the English sentence.

1. *I like to watch TV.* _____

2. *The dog likes to play outside.* _____

3. *Grandfather likes to cook.* _____

4. *Yukari likes to read books.* _____

A. Watashi wa terebi o miru no ga suki desu.

B. Yukari wa hon o yomu no ga suki desu.

C. Inu wa soto de asobu no ga suki desu.

D. Ojīsan wa ryōri o suru no ga suki desu ka.

PRACTICE

Use the picture to help you fill in the blanks with:

ni, no shita ni, no yoko ni, no ushiro ni, no ue ni

1. Ojīsan wa beddo _____ imasu.

2. Neko wa beddo _____ imasu

3. Hon wa kāpetto _____ arimasu.

4. Mado wa beddo _____ arimasu.

5. Omocha wa beddo _____ arimasu.

Now write 2 sentences of your own describing the picture.

1. _____.

2. _____.

CHAPTER 12

Shūmatsu wa dō deshita ka
How was your weekend?

Uso deshō.
You're lying!
(you must be joking)

Shigoto o shinakute wa
ikemasen
must do work

Saikō deshita.
It was great! (the best)

Hontō desu.
It's the truth.

Getsu-yōbi no asa desu. Kubota san wa Yamada San no dōryō desu. Kubota san wa
co-worker

Yamada San to hanashite imasu.
are talking (hanasu)

Kubota: Yamada san, ohayō gozaimasu.

Yamada: Ohayō gozaimasu.

Kubota: Shūmatsu wa dō deshita ka.
weekend

Yamada: Tanoshikatta desu yo.
was fun

Kubota: Nani o shimashita ka.

Yamada: Do-yōbi wa imōto to tenisu o
play tennis

shimashita. Sono ban Rōringu
evening   Rolling Stones

Stōnzu no konsāto ni ikimashita.
go to a concert

Saikō deshita.

70

Kubota: Watashi mo Rōringu Stōnzu ga daisuki desu. Demo, mada konsāto o yatte iru

to be doing;
yarimasu=to do/play/make

nan te bikkuri shimasu ne.

to be surprised

Yamada: Sō desu ne. De mo, mada sugoi desu yo. Kubota san wa shūmatsu ni

nani o shimashita ka. Itsumo no yō ni sakkā o shimashita ka.

as always

Kubota: Hai, do-yōbi ni wa sakkā o shimashita. Kinō wa basuketto shimashita.

Yūbe wa oi to ēga o mimashita.

last night nephew to see a movie

Yamada: Nan no ēga desu ka.

Kubota: Harī Pottā desu.

Harry Potter

Yamada: Yokatta desu ka.

Kubota: Hai, yokatta desu yo. Watashi no oi wa

nana sai na no de kowagatte imashita ga,

because   looked scared

watashi ni wa omoshirokatta desu.

Yamada: Watashi wa romanchikku na ēga no hō ga ī desu.

romantic

Kubota: Sō desu ka. Watashi mo.

Yamada: Hē. Uso deshō.

Kubota: Hontō desu yo. A, mō shigoto o shinakute

knows/understands already

wa ikemasen. Mata, Asa no kaigi

meeting

de aimashō.

let's meet/see you there (au)

Yamada: Asa no kaigi. Wasurete imashita.

Match the questions and statements on the left with the appropriate responses on the right.

a) Shūmastu wa tanoshikatta desu.
b) Sakkā o shimashita.
c) Saikō deshita.
d) Hontō desu.
e) Nan no ēga o mimashita ka.
f) Hai. Yokatta desu.

_____ 1. Yokatta desu ka.
_____ 2. Harī Pottā o mimashita.
_____ 3. Uso deshō.
_____ 4. Shūmastu wa dō deshita ka.
_____ 5. Konsāto wa dō deshita ka.
_____ 6. Shūmastu ni nani o shimashita ka.

THE KEY TO JAPANESE VERBS

Here is your Rosetta Stone for unlocking Japanese's two verb groups, ru and u, and two irregular verbs. You'll notice that the infinitive form – that's the one you'll find listed in the dictionary – always ends with some kind of '–u' sound. You'll often hear the dictionary form used as–is in informal speech in Japan, but we recommend you play it safe and focus on the safe and standard masu forms.

GROUPS		RU	U	IRREGULAR	
Examples		taberu *to eat* miru *to see* neru *to sleep* akeru *to open*	kaku *to write* yomu *to read* iku *to go* kau *to buy* hanasu *to speak* nomu *to drink*	kuru *to come*	suru *to do*
Dictionary form		taberu	kaku	kuru	suru
Plain	present	taberu	kaku	kuru	suru
	negative	tabe + nai	kaka + nai	konai	shinai
	past	tabe + ta	kai + ta	kita	shita
	negative	tabe + nakatta	kaka + nakatta	konakatta	shinakatta
Polite	present	tabe + masu	kaki + masu	kimasu	shimasu
	negative	tabe + masen	kaki + masen	kimasen	shimasen
	past	tabe + mashita	kaki + mashita	kimashita	shimashita
	negative	tabe + masen deshita	kaki + masen deshita	kimasen deshita	shimasen deshita
	'TE' form	tabe + te	kai + te	kite	shite

'te' form of 'u' verbs:

kiku (hear) → ki + ite

oyogu (swim) → oyo + ide

hanasu (speak) → hana + shite

nomu (drink) → no + nde

tobu (fly) → to +nde

toru (take) → to +tte

matsu (wait) → ma + tte

kau (buy) → ka +tte

*iku (go) → itte

EXAMPLES:

plain present:	Pan o taberu. *(I) will eat bread.*
negative:	Bīru o nomanai. *(I) don't drink beer.*
plain past:	Aki ni Nihon ni kita. *(I) came to Japan in autumn.*
negative:	Nani mo shinakatta. *(I) didn't do anything.*
polite present:	Tanaka san wa mainichi oyogimasu. *Ms. Tanaka swims everyday.*
negative:	Suzuki san wa ēgo o hanashimasen. *Mr. Suzuki does not speak English.*
polite past:	Haha wa ēga ni ikimashita. *My mother went to the movie.*
negative:	Sensē wa kimasen deshita. *The teacher didn't come.*
te form:	Tenisu o shite imasu. *(He) is playing tennis.*
	Tabete kudasai. *Please eat.*

About the **'te'** form:

Though **te** form has a number of uses,
two primary ones are:

present progressive:	tonde imasu	*is flying*
	tabete imasu	*is eating*
polite requests:	kiite kudasai	*please listen*
	matte kudasai	*please wait*

***iku** is a regular 'u' verb whose 'te' form is an exception.

Use **–tai** to say 'I want to':

In Japanese you can say "I want to _____." by adding **tai** to the same verb stem you would use for **masu.** When using **–tai** you should add **desu** at the end to make it more polite. (You don't want to sound like a demanding child!) Also note the difference for first person (**–tai desu**) and third person (**–tagatte imasu**).

	First person	Third person
iku → iki + masu	iki + tai Watashi wa Nihon ni ikitai desu. *I want to go to Japan.*	iki + tagatte imasu Maeda san wa Amerika ni ikitagatte imasu. *Mr. Maeda wants to go to America.*
taberu → tabe + masu	tabe + tai Sushi o tabetai desu. *I want to eat sushi.*	tabe + tagatte imasu Sensē wa piza o tabetagatte imasu. *Teacher wants to eat pizza.*

FOCUS: PAST TENSE

In Japanese, the past tense of words falls into 3 basic categories: words accompanied by **desu** such as question words, **na** adjectives, and nouns; **i** adjectives (and adverbs); and verbs. In the past tense all three forms end in **'ta'** For example, this chapter introduced **'yokatta desu'** (I adjective). **'Ēga o mimashita'** (verb), and **'dō deshita ka'** (question word).

To form the past tense of **desu,** you change **'desu'** to **'deshita'**.
kirē desu   kirē deshita *(was pretty)*
Ikura desu ka.   Ikura deshita ka. *(how much was it?)*

To form the past tense of **i** adjectives you take off the final **'i'** and add **'katta'**
tanoshī (tanoshii) desu   tanoshikatta desu *(was fun)*
ureshī (ureshii) desu   ureshikatta desu *(was happy)*

To form the past tense of **masu** verbs, you merely replace **'masu'** with **'mashita'**.
tabemasu   tabemashita *(ate)*
ikimasu   ikimashita *(went)*

PRACTICE

Read the following paragraph. Some of the words are missing. Fill-in the blanks with words below, changing them to the past tense.

1. denwa shimasu	2. hanashimasu	3. shimasu
4. mimasu	5. dō desu ka	6. tanoshī desu
7. oyogimasu	8. ikimasu	9. saikō desu

Kinō wa, tomodachi ni _____ .
                                1. telephoned

Nagai aida shūmatsu ni tsuite _____ .
     time/period   *about*   *2. spoke/talked*

Tomodachi: "Do-yōbi no asa sakkā o _____

kara, totemo tuskaremashita.
3. *played/did*

Soshite, nichi–yōbi wa ie de ichi nichi jū terebi o
  all day

_____."
  4. *watched*

Tomodachi: "Shūmastsu wa _____ ka."
  5. *how was it*

Watashi: "_____."
  6. *was fun*

Do-yōbi ni bōifurendo to mizūmi de _____.
  boyfriend   *lake*   7. *swam*

Sono yoru patī ni _____. _____."
  8. *went*   9. *was great*

CHAPTER 13

Nani o tabetai desu ka
What do you want to eat?

Onaka ga peko peko desu
I am very hungry/starving

Kanpai!
Cheers!

Itadakimasu*
**set phrase giving thanks to the host or the*
person that prepared the food, said
before eating. Not religious

nomimono	bīru	kōhī	wain	ocha/ kōcha
beverage	*beer*	*coffee*	*wine*	*green/black tea*

furūtsu
fruit

painappuru
pineapple

sakuranbo
cherries

dezāto
dessert

kēki
cake

ringo
apples

ichigo
strawberries

tamanegi
onions

ame/(o)kashi
candy

pai
pie

banana
bananas

aisukurīmu
ice cream

orenji
oranges

gohan
rice

sakana
fish

miruku
milk

(o) niku
meat

tamago
eggs

toriniku/chikin
poultry

ninjin
carrots

sutēki
steak

masshurūmu
mushrooms

poteto furai
french fries

hamu/ buta niku/
pōku
ham/pork

tomato
tomatoes

sūpu
soup

pan
bread

chīzu
cheese

yasai
vegetables

sarada
salad

edamame
soybeans

Takahashi san to dōryō no Ogura san to Akagi san wa furansu ryōri no resutoran ni imasu.

Takahashi: Nani o tabemasu ka.

Ogura: Sō desu ne. Amari onaka ga suite imasen kara, sūpu to sarada ni shimasu.

will have

Takahashi: Akagi san wa.

Akagi: Watashi desu ka. Watashi wa onaka ga pekopeko desu. Kesa asagohan o

this morning

tabemasen deshita.

Takahashi: Dōshite desu ka.
why

Akagi: Asa nebō o shimashita kara taberu jikan ga arimasen deshita.

Jitsu wa, shigoto ni mo okuremashita.
actually   *to be late*

Ogura: Sore wa ikemasen ne.
That's bad/that's no good. (polite)

Scene 2:   **The waiter comes to the table and asks for their orders.**

Wuētā: Okimari deshō ka.   **Ogura:**   Kyō no hi-gawari sūpu wa nan desu ka.
to decide (kimaru)   *daily special*

Wuētā: Kyō no sūpu wa poteto kurīmu desu.   **Ogura:**   Jā, sore to sarada o kudasai.
potato cream

Wuētā: Hai. Sūpu to sarada desu ne.

Ogura: Sō desu.

Takahashi: Boku wa chīzu omuretsu to tomato sarada o kudasai.
omelet

Wuētā: Omuretsu to tomato sarada desu ne.

Takahashi: Hai, sore to, dezāto ni ichigo shōto kēki o kudasai.
for/as   short cake

Wuētā: Hai, shōto kēki desu ne. Sochira no okyakusama, nani ni nasaimasu ka.

Akagi: Mazu, sūpu. Sorekara, chikin no shirowain mushi
First of all,   steamed

to dezāto ni pudingu o kudasai.
pudding

Wuētā: Mōshiwake gozaimasen. Kyō wa chikin ga chotto.....
I'm sorry. (polite)   *lit. a little.
*Saying "chotto" and letting the sentence hang is a common, polite way to say no or break some bad news.

Sāmon ga osusume desu ga.
salmon   recommendation

Akagi: Sō desu ka. Jā, sāmon o kudasai.

Wuētā: Dezāto wa ikaga desu ka.
*How about… (honorific form of **dō**)*

Akagi: Ichigo aisukurīmu o kudasai.

Takahashi: Sore to, shiro wain o ippon kudasai.
one bottle

Wuētā: Kashikomarimashita.

The wine and food arrive.

San nin: Kanpai.   Itadakimasu.

PRACTICE

Use the clues in English to find the words in **nihongo.**
Hint: If the word has an extended vowel you need to
write it twice in the puzzle **(e.g. kōcha would be koocha)**

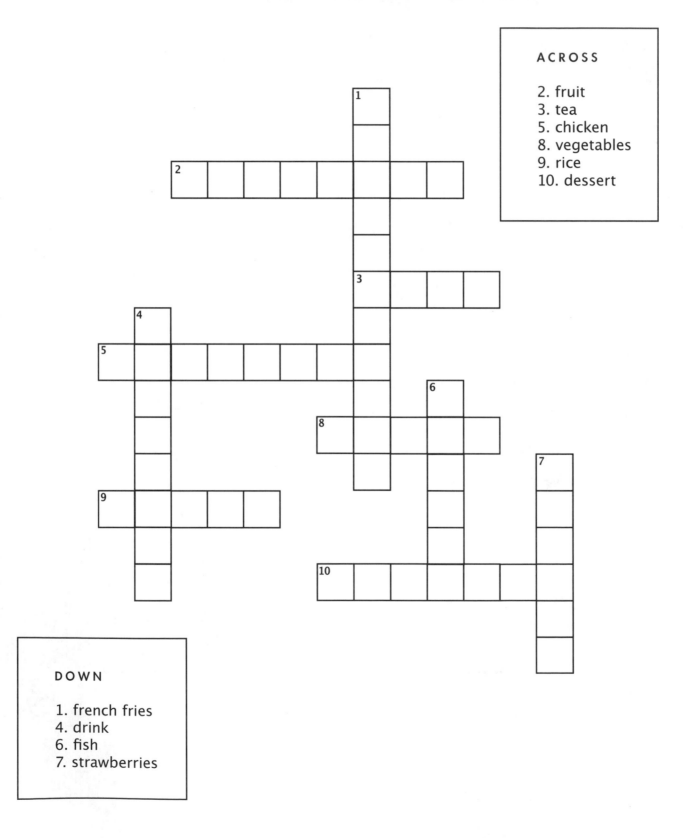

ACROSS

2. fruit
3. tea
5. chicken
8. vegetables
9. rice
10. dessert

DOWN

1. french fries
4. drink
6. fish
7. strawberries

REVIEW

Maru *(true)* or **Batsu** *(false)*

1. Akagi san wa totemo onaka ga suite imashita. _____

2. Ichigo shōto kēki wa dezāto desu. _____

3. Takahashi san wa aka wain o tanomimashita. _____
   asked for/ordered

4. Akagi san wa chikin o tabemashita. _____

5. Akagi san wa chokorēto aisukurīmu ga hoshikatta desu. _____

FOCUS:GRAMMAR

Ko, So, A
here, there, and over there

Japanese are more precise regarding the exact position of something than English speakers. In Japanese the prefixes, *'ko-'*, *'so-'*, and *'a-'* tell you where something is (literally or figuratively) in relation to the speaker. *'Ko-'*, as in **kore** (this thing) is close to the speaker; *'so-'*, as in **sore** (that thing), is far from the speaker and close to the listener; *'a-'*, as in **are** (that thing over there), is far from both speaker and listener. Figuratively, the difference between that and that over there is that *'a-'* refers to a topic that is known or has been previously discussed while *'so-'* refers to a completely new topic.

Look at the explanation below for some of the most commonly used prefixes **ko, so,** and **a.**

	near the speaker	near the listener	far from both
plain pronouns used	kore	sore	are
by themselves	Kore wa pen desu.	Sore wa neko desu.	Are wa inu desu.
pronoun + noun	kono + noun	sono + noun	ano + noun
places (plain)	koko	soko	asoko
places (polite)	kochira	sochira	achira

CHAPTER 14

Dō shimashita ka.
What's the matter? (polite)

Kuta kuta
beat/ I'm exhausted.

Otanjōbi, omedetō gozaimasu.
Happy birthday!

Dō shita no.
What's the matter? (informal)

Kibun ga yokunai.
I don't feel well.

VOCABULARY

(o)iwai *celebrate*	kaze *a cold*	byōki *sick*	kenkō *health*
futorimasu *get fat / gain weight*		Taihen desu. *That's bad./Too bad.*	

DIALOG

Kyō wa Kanako no tanjōbi desu. Tomodachi no Midori no ie de oiwai o shimasu.

Midori: Kanako san, otanjōbi omedetō gozaimasu.

Kanako: Arigatō gozaimasu. Kyō wa ī tenki desu ne. Soto de hiru-gohan

o tabemashō yo.

Midori: Sō desu ne. Niwa de tabemashō.

Midori: Juri san, dō shimashita ka.

Juri: Chotto kibun ga yokunai desu.

Midori: Sore wa ikemasen ne. Kaze desu ka.

Juri: Hai. Nodo ga itai desu.
throat hurts/sore

Midori: Itsu kara kaze desu ka.

Juri: Kinō kara desu.

Midori: Taihen desu ne. Kyō wa daijōbu desu ka.
okay

Juri: Kanako san no tanjōbi desu kara, oiwai ni kimashita.

Kanako: Wazawaza arigatō gozaimasu.
very kind of you

Juri: I e I e. Tokoro de, Kanako san wa genki desu ka. Sengetsu wa byōki deshita ne.
by the way   *last month*

Kanako: Mō genki desu yo. Mite kudasai. Futorimashita.
                       Look please

Juri: Sō desu ka. Shigoto wa dō desu ka.

Kanako: Me ga mawaru hodo isogashī desu ga, naka naka omoshiroi desu.
makes my eyes spin

Mainichi ironna hito to aimasu kara ne.
                   variety of people

84

Juri: Ī desu ne.

Midori: Hai, minasan oshokuji desu. Kyō wa poteto sarada to kara-age to
everyone   *fried chicken*

pasuta to bāsudē kēki desu yo. Mazu, kanpai shimashō.
birthday cake   *first*

San nin: Kanpai.

**Midori,
Juri:** Kanako san no san-jū-go sai no otanjōbi ni.

Kanako: Juri san no kenkō ni.

Juri: Mō sukkari kibun ga yoku narimashita.
      completely   *got better*

YES OR NO?

Read in *ēgo*. Answer in *nihingo.*

1. Does Juri have a sore throat?   _____

2. Does Kanako like her job?   _____

3. Is the celebration at Juri's house? _____

4. Is it Kanako's thirtieth birthday? _____

5. Was Kanako sick last month?   _____

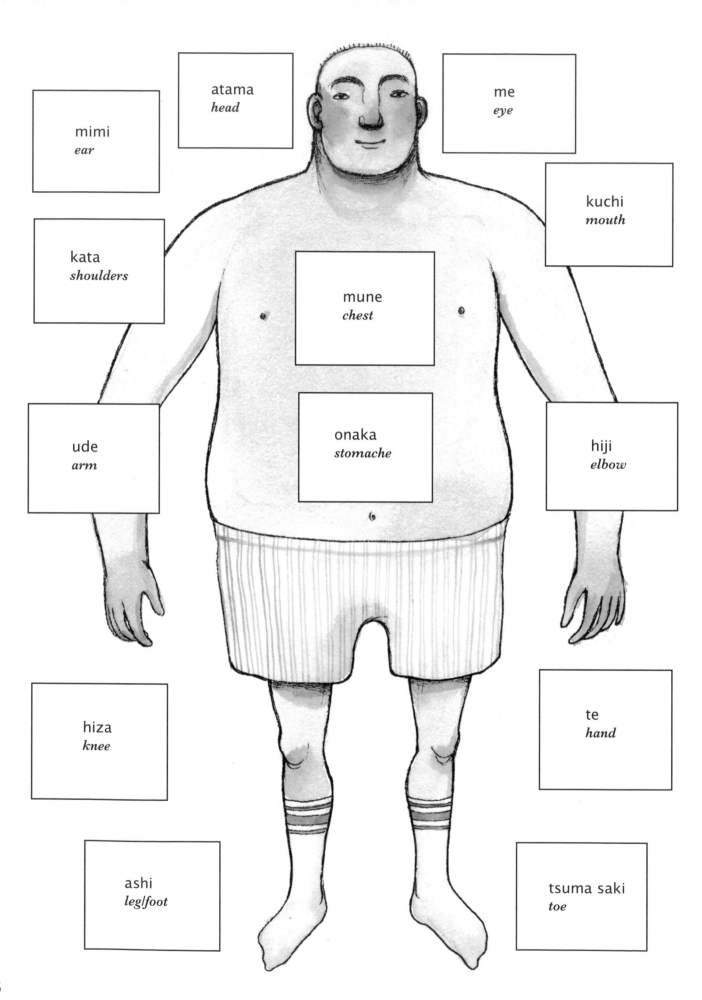

mimi
ear

atama
head

me
eye

kuchi
mouth

kata
shoulders

mune
chest

ude
arm

onaka
stomache

hiji
elbow

hiza
knee

te
hand

ashi
leg/foot

tsuma saki
toe

PRACTICE

In Japanese, the simplest way to express that somewhere hurts is to say _____ *ga itai desu.* If you want to say that you have a cold, are sick, or have some specific illness, you would say _____ *desu.*

Remember that Juri said, "I have a sore throat." See if you can match *ego* with *nihongo* by looking at the diagram. Write the letters in the blanks

1. Onaka ga itai desu.   _____   a. My feet hurt.

2. Hiza ga itai desu.   _____   b. My eyes hurt.

3. Atama ga itai desu.   _____   c. I have a stomachache.

4. Ashi ga itai desu.   _____   d. My neck hurts.

5. Mimi ga itai desu.   _____   e. My knee hurts.

6. Me ga itai desu.   _____   f. I have a headache.

7. Kubi ga itai desu.   _____   g. I have an earache.

ONOMATOPOEIA IN JAPANESE

Japanese abounds with *gitaigo* and *giongo* (onomatopoeia), especially when it comes to expressing emotions and feelings. There are thousands of these expressions, or phrases, and they are part of everyday speech. English examples would be ding, dong or drip, drip, but the Japanese *gitaigo* and *giongo* go far beyond what we have in English to represent weather, emotions, physical conditions and just about anything.

Gitaigo and *Giongo* for Pain

Doko ga itai desu ka.

Onaka ga chiku chiku shimasu.	a sharp pain, like needles, in the stomach
Atama ga gan gan shimasu.	a pounding headache
Te ga hiri hiri shimasu.	burning sensation in the hand(s)
Ashi ga zuki zuki shimasu.	throbbing leg(s)
Muka muka shimasu.	nausea
Fura fura shimasu.	dizzy, shaky, tired

CHAPTER 15

Niamasu yo.
That suits you!

Zettai dame desu
No way!

Daijōbu (desu yo).
It's okay./Don't worry.

Sēru ni natte imasu.
On sale.

VOCABULARY

burajā
bra

kimono
*traditional Japanese dress,
made of silk or cotton*

pantsu/shitagi
underpants/undershirts

mizugi
swimsuit

kaban
purse

jaketto
jacket (sport)

sunīkā
tennis shoes/ sports shoes

tebukuro
gloves

han zubon/shōto pantsu
shorts

t-shatsu
t-shirt

doresu
dress

kutsushita
socks

torēnā
sweats

jīpan
jeans

fujin fuku
women's wear

bōshi
hat

shinshi fuku
men's wear

rēn kōto
raincoat

burezā
blazer

sukāfu
*scarf
(around neck)*

nekutai
tie

kōto
coat

sūtsu
suit

sukāto to
burausu to sētā
*skirt & blouse &
sweater*

zubon to shatsu
pants & shirt

būtsu
boots

kasa
umbrella

DIALOG

NOTE: *You may need to review the colors in chapter 5*

Nagahama Yasushi to Onishi Ritusko wa shucchō de Hawai ni ikimasu. Sono tame no yōfuku
for that purpose clothing

o kaimasu. Ima wa depāto no shinshi fuku uriba ni imasu. Yasushi wa gurē no sūtsu o
  to buy (kau)   department

shichaku shite imasu.
trying on (for size)

Ritsuko: Sono sūtsu, pittari desu kedo irimasu ka. Watashi wa sūtsu o
                      fits well
                motte ikimasen yo.
                will not bring: motte= te of mochimasu (motsu)

Yasushi: Sō desu ne. Hawai no mītingu ni wa katasugimasu ne.
                                meeting   too formal

Ritsuko: Kono zubon to pinku no shatsu o shichaku shite mitara dō desuka.
                                                        try it and see

Yasushi: Pinku desu ka. Zettai dame desu. Ao no shatsu ga ī desu.

*Sales person enters. Sales person is **ten-in** in Japanese.*

Ten-in: Irasshaimase.

Yasushi: Sumimasen. Ao no shatsu wa arimasu ka.

Ten-in: Sono saizu de yoroshī deshō ka.

Yasushi: Hai.

Ten-in: Kochira desu.

Yasushi: Ā, kore ga ī desu. Sore to, jaketto mo sagashite imasu.

to look for (sagasu)

Ten-in: Kore wa sēru ni natte imasu ga.

Ritsuko: Kakko ī desu ne. Niaimasu yo.
Cool/trendy

Yasushi: Yokatta. Jā, kono zubon to ao no shatsu to kono

jaketto o kudasai.

Ten-in: Kashikomarimashita. Oshiharai wa sochira ni narimasu.
payment/paying

Sorekara, Yasushi to Ritsuko wa fujin fuku uriba ni imasu.

Ritsuko wa kīro no doresu o shichaku shite imasu.

Yasushi: Sono doresu wa kirē desu ga, chotto ōkī desu ne.

Ritsuko: Sō desu ne. Sumimasen. Kono doresu no 'S' saizu wa arimasu ka.
small

Ten-in: Mōshiwake arimasen ga, saizu wa sore dake desu.
only that/that's all

Yasushi: Kono aka no doresu wa dō desu ka.

Ritsuko: Sono doresu wa chotto....

Yasushi: Daijōbu. Hoka ni mo arimasu yo.
others

Ten-in: Jā, kono sukāto wa ikaga desu ka. Saizu mo ī to omoimasu.
to think, believe (omou)

Ritsuko: Ī desu ne.

Yasushi: Shichaku shite mitara dō desu ka.

Ten-in: Kochira no shatsu to sukāfu wa sono sukāto ni yoku aimasu yo.
good match

Ritsuko: Sō desu ka. (to Yasushi) Dō deshō ka.

Yasushi: Suteki desu yo.
Great/fabulous

Ritsuko: Yokatta. Jā, kore kara mizugi o kai ni ikimashō.
go and buy; stem ni ikimasu: go and...
Sorede Hawai no junbi wa ōkē desu ne.
preparations okay

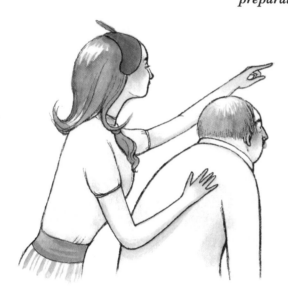 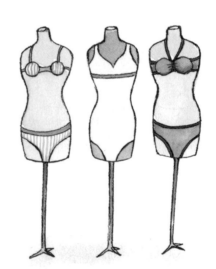

WAKARIMASU KA

Which of these statements describe the situations in the dialogs? Put a check next to the sentences that are true.

1. _____ Yasushi wa pinku no shatsu o kaimasu.

2. _____ Ritsuko wa sukāto ga suki desu.

3. _____ Ritsuko wa aka no doresu ga suki desu.

4. _____ Yasushi to Ritsuko wa Hawai ni ikimasu.

5. _____ "Doresu wa chīsai desu ne." to Yasushi ga īmasu.

Each of the 8 words below is a scrambled word for a piece of women's clothing or accessory. Unscramble each of the clue words. Copy the letters in the numbered cells to other cells with the same number. Then you will find the answer to the question!

HINT: long vowels should be written twice *(e.g. sūtsu suutsu)* (The answer does not refer to the dialogs in this chapter.)

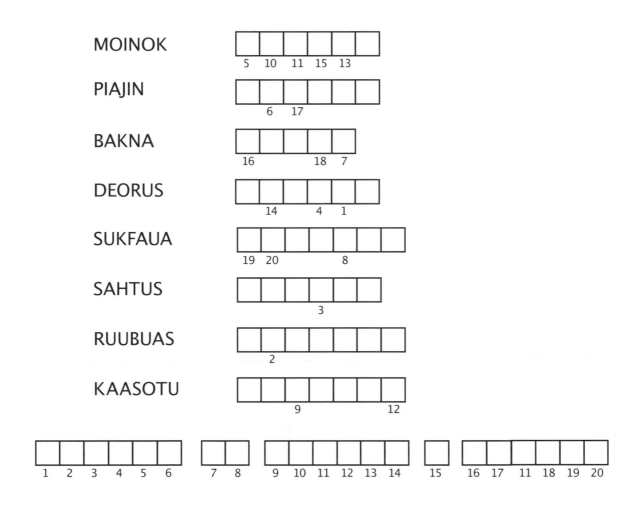

MOINOK | 5 10 11 15 13

PIAJIN | 6 17

BAKNA | 16 18 7

DEORUS | 14 4 1

SUKFAUA | 19 20 8

SAHTUS | 3

RUUBUAS | 2

KAASOTU | 9 12

1 2 3 4 5 6 — 7 8 — 9 10 11 12 13 14 — 15 — 16 17 11 18 19 20

FOCUS

HOW DO YOU WEAR IT?

Unlike in English where you 'wear' almost any article of clothing, in Japanese the verb 'to wear' changes depending on what kind of object you put on.

	PUT ON	TAKE OFF
hat	kaburimasu (kaburu)	torimasu (toru)
glasses	kakemasu (kakeru)	torimasu (toru)
clothing for upper body	kimasu (kiru)	nugimasu (nugu)
clothing for lower body	hakimasu (haku)	nugimasu (nugu)
accessories	shimasu (suru)	torimasu (toru)

CHAPTER 16

Shikata ga nai.
There is nothing to be done./That's life.

No matter how much you prepare for a **ryokō** to a **gaikoku** (foreign country), there will often be some unexpected things that can happen. When some of these things are unfortunate or unpleasant, it helps to know some of the **kotoba** (language) in order to **wakarimasu** what people (like doctors or police) are asking. You might also need to **setsumei** (explain) what happened. A good attitude goes a long way in preparing you to cope with unfortunate circumstances. Accepting an unforeseen event as part of your **kēken** (experience) will help you get through it. You will see in the story in this chapter how Robert, from New York, handles his **mondai** (problems) on a business trip to Nagoya.

tsuite imasen
unlucky (lit. luck doesn't stick.)

tsuite imasu (tsuku)
lucky (lit. luck sticks.)

nusumaremasu (nusumu)
to have something stolen

gamen
screen (computer)

koshō shimasu (koshō suru)
to be broken/out of order

purintā
printer

fakkusu
fax

konpyūta/pasokon
computer

denwa
telephone

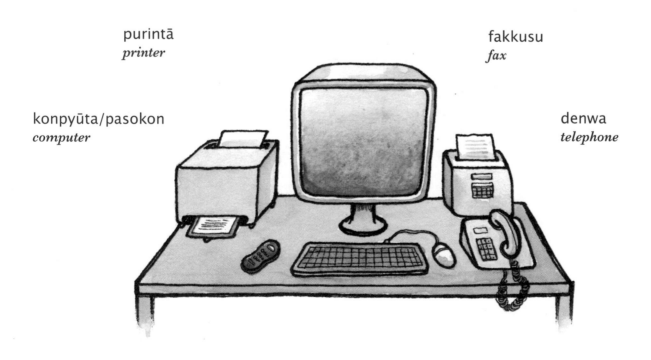

kētai (denwa)
cellphone

kībōdo
keyboard

mausu
mouse

STORY

Watashi no ani no Robāto wa tsuite imasen. Ani wa sengetsu shucchō de Nagoya ni ikimashita.
last month

Mazu, kūkō de pasokon o nusumarete shimaimashita.   Kawaisō ni.
airport   *ended up/regrettably happened*

Nyū Yōku no jimusho ni fakkusu o okurimashita ga todokimasen deshita.
New York   office   fax   sent (okuru)   did not arrive/did not reach

Jimusho no rusuban denwa mo koshō shite imashita.
answering machine

Tsugi no hi, mītingu ni iku tochū   michi ni mayotte shimaimashita. Soshite yon–jū–go
next day   meeting   on the way   lose the way; get lost

fun mo okurete shimaimashita.
okuremasu(okureru)

Hoteru no chikaku de intānetto kafe o mitsukete, kachō to kazoku to tomodachi ni
(chikai) close to internet café (mitsukeru) find section chief

Ī-mēru o okuru koto ga dekimashita. Maiban sono kafe no konpyūta o tsukaimashita.
able to send   every evening   (tsukau) to use

Kafe ni wa hito ga takusan imashita.

95

Minna Ī-mēru o kaitari, webusaito o mitari, wāpuro o tsukattari shite imashita.
word processer tsukau

Nihon no kībōdo wa Amerika no to chigaimasu kara amari hayaku kakemasen deshita.
(chigau) to be different   wasn't able to write

Aru hi Robāto wa mausu to kībōdo ni kōhī o koboshite shimaimashita.
one day

Soshite, kawaisō ni, ōnā ni okorarete shimaimashita.
owner   (okoru) get angry
the owner got angry at him

Doyōbi wa tenki ga yokatta no de, renta-kā o karimashita. Doraibu ni iku tsumori deshita
rental car   (kariru) borrow/rent drive   to intend

ga, tochū de kuruma ga koshō shite shimaimashita. Hontō ni tsuite imasen deshita.

Nichiyōbi wa jitensha o karite, chikaku no ōki na kōen ni ikimashita.
           bicycle   *big*

Demo, hotondo ame de kaeri ni wa taiya ga panku shite shimaimashita. Hontō ni
     nearly (whole time) *on the return trip tire   get a puncture/flat tire*

kawaisō deshita. Demo, sonna ni tsuite inai toki demo, ani wa "shikata ga nai" to īmasu.
                   that much   *time*

WAKARIMASU KA

Match the phrases on the left with the words on the right.

1. Yon-jū-go fun mo okurete shimaimashita. _____   a) mausu to kībōdo

2. Jimusho ni todokimasen deshita. _____   b) intānetto kafue

3. Koshō shite shimaimashita. _____   c) mītingu

4. Kōhī o koboshimashita. _____   d) pasokon

5. Taiya ga panku shite shimaimashita. _____   e) kuruma

6. Ī-mēru o okuru koto ga dekimashita. _____   f) jitensha

7. Nusumaremashita. _____   g) fakkusu

MATCHING

Did you notice how often the word **shimaimashita** was used in this story? Following the **'-te'** form of a verb, this means ended up happening, or happened without wanting it to. It almost always has a negative connotation and implies that something bad, out of the speaker's control, has happened. See if you can match the **'-te shimaimashita** form of the verb with the meaning. Look back at the story for help

1. Panku shite shimaimashita. _____   a) Ended up being late

2. Koboshite shimaimashita. _____   b) Ended up being stolen

3. Mayotte shimaimashita. _____   c) Ended up breaking down

4. Koshō shite shimaimashita. _____   d) Ended up getting a flat tire

5. Okurete shimaimashita. _____   e) Ended up getting lost

6. Nusumarete shimaimashita. _____   f) Ended up spilling

7. Okorarete shimaimashita. _____   g) Ended up with someone mad at him

FOCUS

EMERGENCIES

Japan is a relatively safe country, with a much lower
crime rate compared to most. Travelling and walking
late at night is usually safe, although you should
still be cautious. Petty crime is also relatively low
but in crowded trains and subways you should be
more careful. On the other hand, keep a close eye on
your umbrella and bike. These are often 'borrowed'–
umbrellas mistakenly taken and bikes often being
returned later. However, if something more serious occurs,
call 110 for the police and 119 for the ambulance and/or
fire department. Additionally, in every neighborhood is
a **koban,** police box. The police may not speak English but will
certainly try to help you resolve your problem. Medical services in Japan are modern and
efficient and in big cities you will usually find English speaking doctors. Check with your
embassy or consulate for a list of these. Finally, in big cities such as Tokyo, Yokohama,
Kyoto, and Osaka there are free telephone services that will assist with interpretation for
medical or other emergencies. A guidebook or your hotel should have these listed.

Abunai!	Dō shimashista ka.
Danger!/Watch out!	*What happened?*
Tasukete!	_____ o nusumaremashita.
Help!	*My_____ was stolen.*
yakkyoku	Jiko ga arimashita.
pharmacy	*I had /there was an accident…*
kēsatsu	Kyūkyūsha o yonde kudasai!
police	*Call the ambulance!*
Kaji!	_____ o nakushimashita.
fire!	*I've lost my_____.*

Be sure to use the accompanying "phrase" stickers to practice what you've learned.
Place them around your work and home. Build on the foundation this book provides by
immersing yourself in Japanese as much as you can. Listen to audiocassettes and CD's
and interact with CD-Rom products such as those from Topics Entertainment, which are
good sources of authentic Japanese speech. Japanese radio and television programs may
be available in your area while Japanese films and animation are another enjoyable way to
hear the language. Read anything you can find in Japanese, especially manga (Japanese
comic books) that have little kanji and are for all ages. Search the Internet for Japanese
web sites that will give you countless opportunities to read and listen to Japanese. Talk
to Japanese tourists, students, or business people you meet in your country. They will be
pleasantly surprised to hear you speak Japanese! Finally, get in a Japanese mood! Study a
Japanese traditional art, go eat sushi, play a Japanese video game, whatever it takes… but
have fun learning!

ANSWER KEY

CHAPTER 1

Practice *p. 8*
1. bangohan,tabemasu
2. asagohan, de
3. hirugohan, ka
4. doko

Matching *p. 9*
1. A   2. F   3. C   4. B   5. E   6. D

CHAPTER 2

Practice *p. 13*
1. yon or shi
2. jū
3. go
4. san
5. ichi
6. nana or shichi
7. hachi
8. kyū or ku

Do you understand? *p. 15*
1. Satomi to tomodachi wa resutoran de tabete imasu
2. Fumiko wa sandoicchi o futatsu motte imasu
3. Tomo wa resutoran ni hairimasu.
4. Tomo wa totemo ureshisō desu.

CHAPTER 3

Practice *p. 19*
1.   Oikutsu desu ka.
2.   Dochira kara irasshaimashita ka.
3.   Onamae wa nan desu ka.
4.   Ēgo o hanasemasu ka.

Practice *p. 21*
1.   (Your own age) sai desu.
2.   (Your own name) desu.
3.   (Your country or State name) kara kimashita.
4.   (Your own age) sai desu.
5.   Watashi wa (Your own name) desu.
6.   (Your country or State name) kara desu.

CHAPTER 4

Wakarimasu ka *p. 25*
1.   Masako wa nihonjin desu.
2.   Nihongo o sukoshi wakarimasu. Amerikajin desu.
3.   Kurowassan o futatsu..
4.   Masako.
5.   Panya.

Okimari deshō ka: What would you like? *p. 27*
1. jū–ichi
2. jū–hachi
3. jū–go
4. san
5. go
6. ni

CHAPTER 5

Practice: *p. 31*
1. house 2. years old 3. nice 4. a business woman/company employee
5. job. 6. train 7. car

IRO: Crossword Puzzle *p. 32*
Across
2. kuro
6. midori
8. shiro
9. gurē

Down
1. aka
3. orenji
4. chairo
5. ao
7. pinku

Practice *p. 33*
Put the (yōbi) in their correct order by putting a number from 1–7 in front of each day.

4. Sui-yōbi   1. Nichi-yōbi   3. Ka-yōbi   6. Kin-yōbi   2. Getsu-yōbi
7. Do-yōbi   5. Moku-yōbi

CHAPTER 6

Ordinal Numbers *p. 37*

A is ichiban	F is rokuban
B is niban	G is nanaban
C is sanban	H is hachiban
D is yonban	I is kyūban
E is goban	J is jūban

Wakarimasu ka *p. 39*
1. Īe 2. Hai 3. Īe 4. Hai.

CHAPTER 7

Story *p. 42*
1. My mother goes to the ocean in the summer
2. My father goes to the mountains in the winter
3. My younger brother goes hiking in the fall.
4. My younger sister and I pick flowers in the spring.

Practice *p. 44*

A.
1. My father likes winter.
2. My younger brother, Scott, likes hiking.
3. When does my family take trips?
4. Sometimes (we) also go hiking in the winter and spring.

B.
1. Ni-jū-ni sai desu
2. Otōto wa yama ga suki desu.
3. Watashi mo haru ga ichiban suki desu.
4. Roku-gatsu to shichi-gatsu to hachi-gatsu ni wa umi ni ikimasu.

Loan Words *p. 45*

I.	girl	B.	boyfriend
F.	beach	H.	wake-up call
G.	family doctor	A.	off-season
J.	cheese	D.	apartment building
C.	car navigation system	E.	new release movie

CHAPTER 8

Practice *p. 49*

1.	a) Hiroshi	b) Onīsan
2.	a) Shinko	b) Rie san no Onēsan
3.	a) Yoshihisa	b) Otōsan
4.	a) Nobuko	b) Okāsan
5.	a) Rie	b) Okusan

6.   a) Mayumi   b) Giri no Okāsan
7.   a) Kenichiro   b) Giri no Otōsan
8.   a) Saori   b) Musumesan

Give it a try! *p. 50*

kurokunai; nagakunai; hosokunai

Practice *p. 51*
1. se ga takai okāsan
2. kirē na musumesan
3. tanoshī goshujin
4. Obāsan wa omoshiroi desu.
5. Haikingu ga suki de wa arimasen.
6. Hansamu na ojisan

CHAPTER 9

Practice: Wakarimasu ka *p. 55*
1.   Makiko. Makiko ga samui desu.
2.   Alaska. Makiko wa arasuka ni imasu.
3.   Fukuoka. Fukuoka de ame deshita.
4.   Every day except Sunday. Nichi–yobi igai wa mainichi shigoto.
5.   Summer. Natsu ni ikitai.

More Practice *p. 55*

Oksan: 1, 4, 6   Makiko: 2, 3, 5, 7, 8

Practice: Nihon no tenki wa dō desu ka. *p. 56*
1. atsui desu.   2. ame desu.   3. Ī tenki desu.
4. Yuki desu.   5. Kaze desu.   6. tenki ga warvi desu

Practice and Review *p. 57*
1. natsu   2. samui   3. takusan   4. kochira   5. haru

CHAPTER 10

Practice: Wakarimasu ka *p. 61*
1. False 2. True 3. False 4. False 5. True

Practice *p. 62*
1. d 5:30   2. e 9:47   3. a 10:15   4. c 11:38   5. b 4:45

CHAPTER 11

Wakarimasu ka *p. 68*
1. D 2. C 3. E 4. B 5. A

Write the Letter *p. 68*
1. A 2. C 3. D 4. B

Practice *p. 69*
1. ni
2. no ue ni
3. no ue ni
4. No ura ni
5. No shita ni

CHAPTER 12

Matching *p. 72*
1.f 2.e 3.d 4.a 5.c 6.b

Practice *p. 74*
1. Denwa shimashita 2. Hanashimashita 3. Shimashita. 4. Mimashita. 5. Dō deshita ka
6. Tanoshikatta desu. 7. Oyogimashita. 8. Ikimashita. 9. Saikō deshita.

CHAPTER 13

Puzzle: Food Vocabulary *p. 80*

Across
2. furūtsu
3. ocha
5. toriniku
8. yasai
9. gohan
10. dezāto

Down
1. poteto furai
4. nomimono
6. sakana
7. ichigo

Practice: Maru or Batsu *p. 81*
1. Maru 2. Maru 3. Batsu. Shiro wain o tanomimashita. 4. Batsu. Sāmon o tabemashita.
5. Batsu. Ichigo aisukurīmu ga hoshikatta desu.

CHAPTER 14

Yes or No? *p. 85*
1. Hai, nodo ga itai desu.
2. Hai, naka naka omoshiroi desu.
3. Īe, Midori no ie desu.
4. Īe, Kanako no san-jū-go sai no oiwai desu.
5. Hai, sengetsu wa byōki deshita.

Practice *p. 87*
1. C 2. F 3. G. 4. A 5. H 6. B 7. E

CHAPTER 15

Wakarimasu ka *p. 92*

2, 4

Ritsuko wa nani o kimasu ka *p. 93*

Answers:
kimono
jiipan
kaban
doresu
sukaafu
shatsu
burausu
sukaato
Bottom row: suteki na kimono o kimasu (Ritsuko) wears a fabulous kimono

CHAPTER 16

Wakarimasu ka *p. 98*

1. C   2. G   3. E   4. A   5. F   6. B   7. D

Matching *p. 98*

1. d   2. f   3. e   4. c   5. a   6. b   7. G

GLOSSARY

JAPANESE	CHAPTER 1	ENGLISH
Asa		Morning
Asa gohan		Breakfast
Ban gohan		Dinner
Dō desu ka		How about?
Doko de		Where at
Furansu pan		French bread
Furūtsu		Fruit
Hanashimasu		Speak
Hanashite imasu		Are talking
Hiru gohan		Lunch
Hoshī		Want (noun)
Ikimasu		Go
Issho ni		Together
Jā,		Well, then
Ka		Question
Kanojo		She
Kare		He
Kissaten		cafe
ohayō gozaimasu		Good morning
Ohisashiburi		Long time no see
Onna no hito		Woman
Otoko no hito		Man
Sō desu ne		That is right/that is so
Tabemasu		Eat
To		And
Watashi mo		Me too

JAPANESE	CHAPTER 2	ENGLISH
Agemasu		Give
Arigatō gozaimasu		Thank you
Chīzu		Cheeze
Demasu		Leave
Dōzo yoroshiku onegaishimasu		Nice to meet you
Futatsu		Two objects
Hai		Yes
Hairimasu		Enter
Hajimemashite		How do you do?
Hitotsu		One object
Imasu		To be (animate)
Kanashī		Sad
Motte imasu		To have/hold
Ni		In/Into
Onaka ga suite imasu		I'm hungry
Resutoran		Restaurant
Sandoicchi		Sandwich
Shōkai shimasu		introduce
Tomodachi		Friend (s)
Totemo		Very
Ureshī		Happy
Ureshisō		Appears happy

JAPANESE	CHAPTER 3	ENGLISH
Doko/dochira		Where (plain/polite)
Dōzo		Please
Ēgo		English
Hai		Yes
Hanasemasen		Not able to speak
Hanasemasu		Able to speak
Īe		No
Irasshaimasu/irasshaimashita		Come/Came (formal)
Kara		From
Kimasu/kimashita		Come/Came
Kochira wa _____ desu		This is _____
Konnichiwa		Good afternoon
Musuko		Son
Musume		Daugther
Nihongo		Japanese
Oikutsu		How old? Lit. how many
Onamae wa nan desu ka		What is your name?
Onna no hito		Woman
Onna no ko		Girl
Otoko no hito		Man
Otoko no ko		Boy
Sai		Counter for years old
Shū		State

Sukoshi	A little
Sumimasen	Pardon me
Watashi no namae wa _____ desu	My name is _____
Yoroshiku Onegai Shimasu	Nice to meet you

JAPANESE	CHAPTER 4	ENGLISH
Anpan		Sweet bean paste roll
Dō itashimashite		You're welcome
Dōmo arigatō gozaimasu		Thank you very much
En		Yen
Hanashite kudasai		Please speak
Hyaku		Hundred
Irasshaimase		Welcome
Jā mata ne		See you later (informal)
Kekkō Desu		No thanks
Kore o dōzo/ _____ o dōzo		Here this is/ here is noun
Kudasai		Please
Kurowassan		Crossaint
Motto yukkuri		More slowly
Nani ni nasaimasu ka		What will you have? Formal
Nomimasu		Drink
Okimari deshō ka		Have you made a decision
Okyakusama		Customer
Onegaishimasu		Please
Orenji Jūsu		Orange Juice
Panya		Bakery
Sayōnara		Good bye (formal)
Sochira		Over there
Tsugi		Next
Wakarimasen		Not understand
Wakarimashita		Understood
Wakarimasu		Understand

JAPANESE	CHAPTER 5	ENGLISH
Aka		Red
Akaboshi		Red star
Ao		Blue
Chairo		Brown
Chīsa na		Small
Densha		Train
Futari		Two people
Futari to mo		Both of them
Getsu-yōbi		Monday
Hana		Flower
Hito		Person
Hoshi		Star
ī		Nice
Ie		House
Ikimasu		Go
Isogashī		Busy
Kaishain		Company employee/business person
Kin-yōbi		Friday
Kīro		Yellow
Konpyūta puroguramā		Computer programmer
Kuruma		Car
Maishū		Every week
Me		Eye (s)
Midori		Green
Niwa		Garden
Ōki na		Big
Omoshiroi		Interesting
Pinku		Pink
Saite imasu		Blooming
Shigoto		Work
shimasu		Have/do
Shokuji		Meal
Sui-yōbi		Wednesday
Suki		Like
Suki de wa arimasen		Does not like
Sunde imasu		Living
Tanoshī		Fun
To iu/to īmasu		Called/named
Totemo		Very

JAPANESE	CHAPTER 6	ENGLISH
Agaru/Agarimasu		Go up
Aite imasen		Not open
Aite Imasu		To be open

Japanese	English
Arukimasu	Walk
Chikai	Near
ēga	Movie
ēgakan	Movie theater
Fun/pun	Minute
Gurai	About
Hairu/Hairimasu	Enter
Hakubutsukan	Museum
hantai gawa ni	On the other side (of)
Hashi	Bridge
hidari ni	To the left (side)
Ichiban me	First
Ikitai	Want to go
Iku/Ikimasu	Go
Itte kimasu	Set phrase: I come and go.
Itte rasshai	Set phrase: "take care/see you soon"
Kaimono	Shopping
Ki o tsukete	Take care
Kōsaten	Intersection
kyō	Today
Magaru/Magarimasu	Turn
Massugu	Straight ahead
Mazu	First
migi gawa ni	To the right (side)
Ni men shite	facing
No Mukaigawa ni	Across
Noru/Norimasu	Take/ride
Oriru/Orimasu	Go down
Pun/fun	Minute (s) (counter)
Sanpo/Sanpo Shimasu	A Walk/Take a walk
Shimatte Imasu	To be closed
Sore ja	Well then
tōi	far
tōkunai	Not far
tonari ni	Next to/ beside
Tōri/Dōri	Street
Toshokan	Library
tsukiatarimasu	Dead end
Verb te form+ kudasai	Please/polite command for verbs
Wataru/Watarimasu	Cross
Zannen	Too bad

JAPANESE	CHAPTER 7	ENGLISH

Japanese	English
Aki	Autumn
Ane	My Older sister
Ani	My Older brother
Chichi	My Father
Chigaimasu	Different
Daisuki	Like a lot
Dekakeru/dekakemasu	Go out
Fuyu	Winter
Ga	but
Haha	My mother
Haikingu	Hiking
Hana	Flower
Hanami	Flower viewing
Haru	Spring
Ichiban Suki	Favorite/Like the most
Ichinenjū	Year round
Ikitagarimasu	Wants to go; looks like wants to go
Imōto	My Younger sister
Itsu	When
Jitsu wa	The truth is
Kanai/tsuma	My wife
Kara	From
Kazoku	Family
Koto	Thing
Made	To
Minna	Everyone
Minna de	With everyone
Natsu	Summer
Ni-jū-ni sai	22 years old
Number (1-12) + gatsu	January-December
Otōto	My Younger brother
Oya	My Parent (s)
ryokō	Trip
Sate	Well then
Shiawase	happy
Shiki	4 seasons

Japanese	English
Shujin/otto	My Husband
Sore de	That way/therefore
Sukī	Ski/skiing
Tokidoki	Sometimes
Tsumimasu	To pick
Umi	Ocean
Yama	mountain

JAPANESE	CHAPTER 8	ENGLISH
(Se ga) hikui		Short (height)
(Se ga) takai		Tall (height)
Bōshi		Hat
Giri no okāsan		Mother–in–law–honorific
Giri no otōsan		Father–in–law–honorific
Gokazoku		Family –honorific
Goshujin		Husband (not your own)
Hansamu na		Handsome
Hitori		One person
Ippai		Full (of)
Kaburimasu		Wear (hat)
Kami no ke		Hair
Kekkon shite imasu		Is married
kirē		Pretty
Kodomo San		Children/child–honorific
Kuro/kuroi		Black
Megane		Glasses
Mijikai		Short
Nagai		Long
Okāsan		Mother
Okusan		Wife (not your own)
Onēsan		Older sister–honorific
Onīsan		Older brother–honorific
Otōsan		Father
Suteki na		Nice

JAPANESE	CHAPTER 9	ENGLISH
Ame		Rain
Aru/arimasu		Be (inanimate)
Ashita		Tomorrow
Asobi ni kimasu/Kuru		Come play/ hang out
Atsui		Hot
Chō		Town
Da sō		I hear/ apparently
Denwa shimasu		To phone/call
Fuyu yasumi		Winter break
Hare		Sunny/clear
Hidoi		Terrible
Hikōki		Plane
Ī tenki/tenki ga ī		Fine weather
Igai		Except
Ima		Now
Kaeritai		Want to return
Kaeru/Kaerimasu		Return

JAPANESE	CHAPTER 10	ENGLISH	
Ato		After	
Densha		Train	
Eki		Railroad station	
En		Japanese yen	
Ēto		Lets see	story
Fun/pun/bun		Minute	
Hachiban		Number 8	
Ima		Now	
Itsumo		Always	
Kakunin shimasu		To check/confirm	
Katamichi		One–way	
Kippu		Ticket(s)	
Kyūkō		Express train	
Maniaimasu/Maniaimasen		Be on time/ not be on time	
Mō ichi do		Again	
Nanban		What number	
Nanika nomimasen ka		Why don't we drink something	
Noriba		Track	
Ōfuku		Round trip	
Shimatta		Darn	
Sono tsugi		The next	
Tsugi		Next	
Yamete Kudasai		Please stop	
Yuki		Heading to	

JAPANESE	CHAPTER 11	ENGLISH
Asa nebō		Oversleep
Asonderu iru toki		While playing
Beddo		Bed
chīsai		Small/Young(for children)
Daidokoro		Kitchen
Dokusho		Read/reading
Gomibako		Garbage can
Hiku/Hikimasu		Play (an instrument)
Hima na toki		Free time
Hito		Human(s)
Hon		Book
ī –mēru o kakimasu		Write e-mail
Ikkai		1st floor/downstairs
Ima		Living Room
Inu		Dog
Isu		Seat
Kakuremasu		Hide
kawaī		cute
Konpūta		Computer
Kuroneko		Black cat
Mado		Window
Miru/Mimasu		Watch
Neko		Cat
Nemasu		Sleep
Nenpai		Old/elderly (only for people)
Ni kai		2nd floor/upstairs
nin		Counter for people (3 or more)
No mae		Front (of)
No naka		Inside
No shita		Below
No ue		On
No Ushiro		Behind
No yoko		Next to
Node		Because
Ofisu		Office
Omocha		Toy
Oto		Sound
Shinshitsu		Bedroom
Sofā		Sofa
Soto		Outside
Sugoshimasu		Spend time
Suru/Shimasu		Do
Sutōbu		Stove
Suwaru/Suwarimasu		Sit
Terebi		TV
Toranpu		Cards
Tsukemasu		Turn/switch on
Uebusaito o mimasu		Surf the web
Wakai		Young (not used for children)
Yomu/Yomimasu		Read

JAPANESE	CHAPTER 12	ENGLISH
Aimashō		Let's meet
Ban		Evening
Basuketto o shimasu		Play basketball
Bikkuri Shimasu		(Be) surprised
Dōryō		Co-worker
ēga o mimasu		See a movie
Hanashite Imasu		Talking
Kaigi		Meeting
Konsāto ni ikimasu		Go to a concert
Kowagarimasu		Look scared/seem scared
Na no de		Because
Nan te		Somehow
Romanchikku		Romantic
Sakkā o shimasu		Play soccer
Shūmatsu		Weekend
Tenisu o shimasu		Play tennis
Tonoshikatta		Fun (past tense)
Yatte imasu		Doing
Yūbe		Last night

JAPANESE	CHAPTER 13	ENGLISH
(o) niku		Meat
Aisukurīmu		Icecream
Ame/(o)kashi		Candy
Banana		Banana

Japanese	English
Bīru	Beer
Chīzu	Cheese
Dezāto	Dessert
Dōshite	Why
Eda mame	Soy beans
Furūtsu	Fruit
Gohan	Rice
Hamu/Buta niku/pōku	Ham/pork
Hi-gawari	Daily special
Ikaga	How about (formal)
Ippon	One bottle
Jitsu wa	Actually
Kēki	Cake
Kesa	This morning
Kōhī	Coffee
Masshurūmu	Mushrooms
Mazu	First
Miruku	Milk
Ni shimasu	Will have
Ninjin	Carrots
Nomimono	beverage
Ocha/Kōcha	Green tea/tea
Omuretsu	Omelette
Orenji	Oranges
Osusume	Recommend
Pai	Pie
Painappuru	Pineapple
Pan	Bread
Poteto Furai	French fries
Pudingu	Pudding
Ringo	Apple
Sakana	Fish
Sarada	Salad
sarada	salad
Shōto Kēki	Short cake
Sore wa ikemasen	That`s bad/That`s no good
Sūpu	Soup
Sutēki	Steak
Tamago	Eggs
Tamanegi	Onions
Tomato	Tomato
Toriniku/chikin	Chicken
Wain	Wine
Yasai	Vegetables

JAPANESE	CHAPTER 14	ENGLISH
(o)iwai		Celebrate
Byōki		Sick
Futorimasu		Get fat/gain weight
Ironna hito		Variety of people
Itai		Hurt
Kara-age		Fried chicken
Kaze		A cold
Nodo		Throat
Sengetsu		Last month
Soto de		Outside
Sukkiri		Completely
Tokoro de		By the way
Wazawaza		Very kind of you
Yoku narimashita		Got better

JAPANESE	CHAPTER 15	ENGLISH
(O)shiharai		Payment/paying
Basurōbu		Bathrobe
Bōshi		Hat
Burajā		Bra
Burausu		Blouse
Burezā		Blazer
Būtsu		boots
Dansei fuku		Men`s wear
Doresu		Dress
Fujin fuku		Women`s wear
Han zubon/Shōto pantsu		Shorts
Hoka		others
Irimasu		Need
Jaketto		Jacket (sport)
Jīpan		Jeans
Junbi		Preparations
Kaban		Bag
Kai ni ikimashō		Let`s go and buy

Kaimasu	To buy
Kakko ī	Cool/trendy
Kasa	Umbrella
Katasugimasu	Too formal
Kimono	Traditional Japanese silk dress
Kutsu	Shoes
Kutsu shita	Socks
Mītingu	Meeting
Mizugi	Bathing suit
Motte Ikimasu/Ikimasen	Bring/not bring
Nekutai	Necktie
ōkē	Okay
Rēn kōto	Rain coat
Sagasu/Sagashimasu	Look for
Sētā	Sweater
Shatsu	Shirt
Shichaku suru/Shimasu	Try on
Shite mitara/mimashitara	Try and see
Sono tame	For that Purpose
Sore dake	Only that/that's all
Sukāfu	Scarf
Sukāto	Skirt
sunīkā	Tennis shoes/sports shoes
Sūtsu	Suit
Tebukuro	Gloves
To omoimasu	To think/believe
torēnā	Sweats
T–shatsu	T–shirt
Uriba	Department
Yōfuku	Clothing
Yoku aimasu	Good match
Yukata	Cotton Japanese dress
Zubon	Pants

JAPANESE	CHAPTER 16	ENGLISH

Aru hi	One day
Chigaimasu/Chigau	Different
Chikaku	Near
Denwa	Phone
Doraibu	Drive
Fakkusu	Fax
Gamen	Screen (computer)
Hotondo	Nearly (whole time)
Intānetto Kafe	Internet café
Jimusho	Office
Jitensha	Bicycle
kachō	Section chief
Kaeri	Return
Kakemasen deshita	Wasn't able to write
Karimasu/kariru	Rent
Kēitai (denwa)	Cell phone
Kūkō	Airport
Maiban	Every evening
Mausu	Mouse
Michi ni mayotte	Lose the way/get lost
Mītingu	Meeting
Mitsukemasu/mitsukeru	Find
Ni iku tochū	On the way
Nusumaremasu/nusumu	To have something stolen
Ōki	Big
Okoraremasu/okoru	Get angry
Okurimasu/Okuru	Send
Okuru koto ga dekimashita	Able to send
Ōna	Owner
Panku	Get a puncture/flat tire
Purintā	Printer
renta–kā	Rental car
Rusuban denwa	Answering machine
Sengetsu	Last month
Sonna ni	That much
Taiya	Tire
Todokimasen deshita	Did not arrive
Tsugi no hi	Next day
Tsukaimashita/Tsukau	Use
Tsumori	To intend
Wāpuro	Word processor

JAPAN

JAPANESE HOT SPRINGS

Japan is a wonderful place to visit, boasting culture, history, modern conveniences, fabulous food, beautiful nature, and friendly people. The list of tourist sites is long and includes temples and shrines in the ancient capitols of Kyoto and Nara, hiking opportunities in the Japanese Alps or even Mount Fuji, and urban excitement in the cities of Osaka and Tokyo. However, one of the most delightful Japanese experiences is the Onsen, or hot spring.

Japan, a volcanic island, is rich in hot springs, and the Japanese have harnessed these gifts of nature to create one of the most relaxing experiences known to man. Although hot springs can be found in some large cities, they tend to be concentrated in the mountains or close to the sea. According to the Japanese "Hot Spring Bill", a true onsen must be hotter than 77 degrees Farenheit and/or contain a certain amount of over 14 minerals.

WHERE TO FIND ONSENS

Traditionally, hot springs were considered by the Japanese to be therapeutic as well as relaxing. Today, there are approximately 2,000 officially recognized hot springs with the only common denominator being the water temperature and concentration of minerals. You might encounter onsens in the following places:

- A ryokan: A ryokan is a traditional Japanese inn (yet another delightful tourist experience), and many of them have hot spring baths. These may be communal or in a private room.
- Onsen towns: These are towns dedicated to the onsen experience. Expect to see guests walking the streets in their yukata (cotton robes) and geta (wooden sandals) en route to the baths. These towns run the gamut from highly tacky to beautifully traditional.
- A sento (public bath): Public baths are common in Japan. For approximately $4, you can enjoy a HOT bath. In areas rich in hot springs, you can expect the public bath water to be from hot springs!

TYPES OF BATHS

You also might find the following variations of baths:

- Rotenburo: These outdoor onsen are similar to the western jacuzzis but without the bubbles.
- Mud baths: In addition to the pools, vats of beautifying mud are available.
- Tsunaburo (sand baths): Some seaside resorts have sand that is heated by underground vents. You can be buried in hot sand before jumping in the bath.
- Electric pools: To stimulate your health, these baths have a low-level electric current.

Bathing etiquette is taken very seriously in Japan. Some bathhouses have an illustrated guide or instructions in English. The following guidelines were found on the website promoting the famous onsens of Beppu. http://www.welcometobeppu.com/.

- Please remember to wash your body before entering the bathtub.
- Please don't put your towel into the bathtub, because it is not good manners and it would be a nuisance for people who are sharing the bathtub with you.
- Taking a bath for a long time is bad for your health. As soon as your body has become warm and you feel relaxed, step out of the bathtub.
- Please use soap outside of the bathtub, before entering the bathtub.
- After bathing, use your towel to dry your body.

FOOD

Japanese food is more than raw fish. Sushi aficionados might argue that it is the best Japanese dish–but that is for you to decide! 'Ya' means store or restaurant, and you usually tack this onto the food name to indicate that type of restaurant (e.g., a 'sushiya' is a restaurant that serves sushi). Below is a short list of some of the more common dishes and restaurants you might find. Japanese cuisine is truly an adventure, with both inexpensive and astronomically priced gastronomic delights! Explore and enjoy!

Sushi is actually raw fish or vegetables with vinegar-seasoned rice and seaweed, while Sashimi is simply slices of raw fish. Don't expect any deals on sushi/sashimi in Japan, unless you visit what is called 'mawaru sushi' or 'kaitenzushi' (which both mean revolving sushi). This inexpensive type of sushiya serves the food on a conveyer belt. The dishes are color-coded for price–roughly 100–400 yen per plate.

Okonomiyaki might be compared to a western pizza or omelet. The key ingredients are flour, egg, and cabbage, and the customer chooses toppings such as shrimp, pork, cheese, and octopus. The two most famous styles of okonomiyaki are from Osaka and Hiroshima-try both to see which one you like better.

Noodle dishes abound. Do you want them hot or cold, fat or thin, or Chinese- or Japanese-style? Soba are buckwheat noodles, udon are fat, white noodles, ramen are Chinese noodles, and yaki soba (literally, 'grilled soba') are served stir-fried with veggies and a sauce. All of these dishes make a tasty and inexpensive lunch!

Izakayas are Japanese pubs, or tapas bars. You can drink and eat many small dishes in the izakayas until late in the evening. The food generally is grilled (e.g., yakitori, which is grilled chicken on a stick) or fried, and westerners seem to like it.

ETIQUETTE QUIZ

Before reading the information below, find your faux pas
factor in Japan with this maru–batsu (true–false) quiz.

_____ 1) When Japanese bow, their hands form a steeple in front of their faces.
_____ 2) The proper way to enter a Japanese home is to barge in and announce
"onaka ga suite imasu" *(I am hungry)*.
_____ 3) Japanese celebrate Christmas and Valentine's Day.
_____ 4) When not actually using your chopsticks during a meal, it is a common
practice to stick them into your rice.

JAPANESE ETIQUETTE

Japanese behavior is governed by a multitude of rules. Some of these are immediately
apparent to the foreigner (e.g., bowing in greeting), while others may take years to
understand. However, Japanese do not expect foreigners to master all of these rules and
are very gracious in overlooking our mistakes and errors. It is a fact that good intentions
are recognized in every language – smiles are Esperanto. Below are some of the more
important rules of etiquette:

Greeting: It is common knowledge that Japanese bow as a form of greeting. Usually, the
lower the bow, the higher the respect. Women bow with their hands together and to the
front; men bow with their hands to their sides. Bow from the waist, not from the back.
Business people invariably exchange business cards. Accept these with both hands and
pause a moment to view the information.

House Rules: Visiting a Japanese home is a wonderful cultural experience. Always take off
your shoes when entering the house. Usually you would say, 'Shitsurei shimasu' (Excuse
me) or 'Ojama shimasu' (literally, 'I make a nuisance'). Once inside the house you might
be expected to wear slippers. But you must change from house slippers to 'toilet' slippers
when visiting the lavatory. Finally, no slippers are worn on 'tatami,' Japanese mat floors.

Gift Giving: Japanese have traditionally given small gifts to show respect or appreciation,
most notably osēbo (at the end of the year) and ochūgen (in August) to people to whom
they are indebted. Today, gift giving is still alive and well – the department stores are
filled with gifts for Christmas, Valentine's Day (when women give chocolate to boyfriends,
family members, bosses, and any other males in their vicinity), and its Japan–only
counterpart, White Day (when men give chocolate to women). When Japanese go on a
trip, even within Japan, they bring back omiyage (souvenirs) for everyone they know.
Finally, as a visitor you might bring small gifts to give people who help you.

Eating: Japanese do use forks and knifes when eating western food, but chopsticks are
still the main utensils. There are some very serious taboos regarding chopsticks. Never
stick them vertically into rice. Never pass food from chopstick to chopstick. Both of these
are reminiscent of customs performed at funerals. If you are truly trying to 'blend in' at
a formal meal, use one end of your chopsticks to transfer food from a family style plate
to your own, and use the other end to eat. When drinking with Japanese, it is polite to
pour alcohol for others. On the same note, you shouldn't pour your own drink – your
companion will certainly keep your glass full.

Gestures: In Western countries a common gesture meaning 'come here' is to motion with your finger or arm, palm turned upward. In Japan, the common, polite way to call someone over is to extend your arm, palm facing down, and make a scooping motion toward yourself, bending at the wrist. Pointing your index finger to your nose means 'me' or 'I.' Moving your hand in front of you in a chopping motion indicates 'excuse me' when cutting through a crowd or in front of someone.

Quiz Answers: 1) False   2) False   3) True   4) False

SUPER TECH

Sony, Toyota, and Sega are household names throughout the world. These and other Japanese companies lead the market in developing the newest, latest, and greatest in technology products. Some of these products are exported to overseas markets, but many of the newest are sold only to the well-educated and consumer-savvy Japanese "test market." When you visit Japan, you can get a preview of what might be coming your way in the next one to five years! Below are just a few of the latest technology products and related phenomena in Japan.

Mobile Phone Technology: Did you know that three out of five people in Japan own a cell phone—more than own a landline? Did you know that approximately 1.5 million Japanese people can type as many as 100 characters per minute on their cell phones, using only two thumbs? Not only are Japanese cell phones generally smaller and lighter than those in other countries, their technology is usually a few steps ahead. New cell phones offer all the options (and more) of a personal computer; you can Web browse on specially designed sites, download and play music and movies, take photos with a digital camera, and even converse face-to-face with someone far away. "Beam me up, Scottie": the age of Star Trek has arrived. *http://www.jinjapan.org/trends/index.html*

Automobile Technology: In Japan, environmentally friendly technology is not just a buzzword. In 2002, Japanese automobile manufacturers Toyota and Honda were the first to begin commercial sales and leasing of fuel cell (hydrogen powered) vehicles, the newest development in eco-friendly technology. Earlier, Japanese automobile makers initiated a "Voluntary Action Plan" that proposed making 95% or more of all automobile parts recyclable by 2015. As of 2002, over 85% of these parts already were recyclable. *http://e450r.jama.or.jp/e_press*

Toy/Robot Technology: Japan is facing the crisis of an aging population, with a smaller proportion of children. Toy makers have responded by making bigger, better, and higher-tech toys that appeal to the child in adults, as well as to their children. Some examples are Sony's AIBO and Tomy's MicroPets; mechanical pets that respond to voice commands; and Konami video game technology that incorporates voice command and 3-D imagery. *http://www.jinjapan.org/trends/index.html*

Paste these removable stickers around your work and home.
It will re-enforce what you've learned!

Ohayō gozaimasu

Onaka ga suite imasu

Yokatta

Hajimemashite

Dōzo yoroshiku onegaishimasu

Dōmo arigatō gozaimasu

Sumimasen

Tsukaremashita

Nodo ga kawakimashita

Gomen nasai

Watashi no namae wa _____ desu

Konnichiwa

Dochira kara kimashita ka

Eigo o hanasemasu ka

(o)Ikura desu ka

Motto yukkuri hanashite kudasai

Wakarimasen

Dō itashimashite

Kekkō desu

Sayōnara

Jā, Mata ne

_____ wa doko desu ka

Itte kimasu

Itte rasshai

Ki o tsukete

Dono kisetsu ga suki desu ka

Genki

Ganbatte kudasai

Tenki wa dō desu ka

Nan ji desu ka

Mō ichi do onegaishimasu

Nanban noriba desu ka

Hima na toki, nani o shimasu ka

Shūmatsu wa dō deshita ka

Nani o tabetai desu ka

Itadakimasu

Kanpai

Dō shimashita ka

Kibun ga yokunai

Doko ga itai desu ka